What I'm Looking Forward To:
Life After Life After Death

What I'm Looking Forward To:
Life After Life After Death

David Pawson

Anchor Recordings

Copyright © 2021 David Pawson Ministry CIO

The right of David Pawson to be identified as author of this Work has been asserted by him in accordance with the Copyright, Designs and Patents Act 1988.

First published in Great Britain in 2021 by
Anchor which is a trading name of David Pawson Publishing Ltd
Synegis House, 21 Crockhamwell Road,
Woodley, Reading RG5 3LE

No part of this publication may be reproduced or transmitted in any form or by any means, electronic or mechanical, including photocopy, recording or any information storage and retrieval system, without prior permission in writing from the publisher.

**For more of David Pawson's teaching,
including DVDs and CDs, go to
www.davidpawson.com**

**FOR FREE DOWNLOADS
www.davidpawson.org**

**For further information, email
info@davidpawsonministry.com**

ISBN 978-1-913472-26-9

Printed by Ingram Spark

Contents

Forward	I
1. Life after Death	9
2. Between Death and Resurrection	31
3. Resurrection	49
4. Judgment	69
5. Hell	89
6. Further Questions	109

This book is based on a series of talks. Originating as it does from the spoken word, its style will be found by many readers to be somewhat different from my usual written style. It is hoped that this will not detract from the substance of the biblical teaching found here.

As always, I ask the reader to compare everything I say or write with what is written in the Bible and, if at any point a conflict is found, always to rely upon the clear teaching of scripture.

David Pawson 1930 - 2020

FOREWORD

David spent the last year of his life in a Nursing Home. He had a lot of time to think about the future and was ready to meet his Lord and Maker when that day came.

During one particular visit to see David he said to me "The Lord prepared me for a Ministry. I served that Ministry and now it's complete, I'm looking forward to the next stage of my life: Life, after Life, after Death". David said he wished this to be the subject of his one last and parting sermon.

Due to COVID and lockdown we were unable to record David one last time, but we hold in the archives a series of talks on this very topic David gave in the early 1970s in the Millmead Centre Guildford, which form the content of this book.

David gave express wishes that he did not want a memorial service:

"I do not wish to be eulogised, nor put on a pedestal."

He did not want anyone to 'celebrate his life', but said to me that "if we wait until we receive our resurrected bodies, then we can all celebrate together" with Him (JESUS)!

David believed and taught that the moment we die we go to be with our Lord in a disembodied form, to a place which Jesus called 'Paradise', somewhere quite different to our final resting place.

David had no fear of death. In fact quite the opposite, he was 'looking forward with anticipation and excitement to finally meet and be in the presence of Jesus—at last'. In the words written on his Grandfather's gravestone:

"What a meeting!"

David is now able to get the answers to the many, many questions he kept in a file at the bottom drawer of his filing cabinet called:

"I'll know when I get there."

David went to be with our Lord on 23rd May 2020 —

Ascension Day — a day David felt had lost prominence in the Church calendar.

Ascension Day was always important to David. Just a few days before lockdown David asked me:

"You do know the importance of Ascension Day?'

and continued:

"The Church celebrates the crucifixion on a Friday, when Jesus did not die on a Friday, it celebrates His birth at Christmas, when Jesus was not born in December nor did he ever talk of his birth, yet Ascension Day has all but disappeared from the Church calendar."

In answering David's question, quite in awe of David's knowledge, and with fear of getting it wrong, I said that of course I know the importance of Ascension Day. After an awkward pause, I asked him to clarify what specifically he was referring to.

David answered:

"Well if Jesus had not ascended, he could not have sent the Holy Spirit and if He had not sent the Holy Spirit there would have been no Pentecost! And if He had not sent the Holy Spirit, we would not be sitting here right now — in fact we may never have met."

Knowing David was such a privilege. The knowledge he has imparted, in such a clear and understandable form, is a priceless legacy.

I'm looking forward to that day when we can celebrate with him, when we receive our resurrected bodies!

Until then ...His Ministry continues.

Steve

Chapter 1

Life After Death

I want to begin with a passage from the Old Testament:

> It is a wonderful thing to be alive! If a person lives to be very old, let him rejoice in every day of life, but let him also remember that eternity is far longer and that everything down here is futile by comparison. Young man, it's wonderful to be young! Enjoy every minute of it! Do all you want to; take in everything, but realize that you must account to God for everything you do. So banish grief and pain, but remember that youth, with a whole life before it, can make serious mistakes. Don't let the excitement of being young cause you to forget about your Creator. Honor him in your youth before the evil years come—when you'll no longer enjoy living. It will be too late then to try to remember him when the sun and light and moon and stars are dim to your old eyes, and there is no silver lining left among your clouds. For there will come a time when your limbs will tremble with age, your strong legs will become weak, and your teeth will be too few to do their work, and there will be blindness too. Then let your lips be tightly closed while eating when your teeth are gone! And you will waken at dawn with the first note of the birds; but you yourself will be deaf and tuneless, with quavering voice. You will be afraid of heights and of falling—a white-haired, withered old man, dragging himself along: without sexual desire, standing at death's door, and nearing his everlasting home as the mourners go

along the streets. Yes, remember your Creator now while you are young–before the silver cord of life snaps, and the gold bowl is broken; before the pitcher is broken at the fountain and the wheel is broken at the cistern; then the dust returns to the earth as it was, and the spirit returns to God who gave it. (Ecclesiastes 11:7–12:7, Living Bible).

That is a very practical passage from the Old Testament which deals with real life and is not afraid to face the facts. In this chapter and those which follow I am going to be addressing the subject of life after death, and Christians are the only people who can really face up to this subject. Others must face it with questions, doubts, and fears. Christians can face it in the light of Easter. We are going to look at various subjects and aspects of life after death, but before we can do so, we must look very squarely and very directly at the fact of death itself. It is the biggest fact of life. It is the one certain thing that we can predict about the future, and so it is right that we should face death, and look it in the face, and then see it as a conquered enemy. This is what we hope to do in this chapter.

Now to introduce the subject to you, I am going to include an interview with a member of the congregation of a church where I was pastor who was in the medical profession and came to talk about this subject. I suppose that the medical profession sees more of death than most others, perhaps with ministers coming second. Maybe I should put undertakers first and medical professionals second, and maybe ministers third. But nevertheless, we share in common that both of us have had quite a lot to do with death in one way or another. I am going to ask some questions about this to try to help us to face up to the fact, to see it in a Christian light, and to understand something of its meaning.

David: "Now, as a member of the medical profession, you've seen quite a lot of death. In fact, you've seen more of death than perhaps many members of the congregation. I'd like to ask you if your reaction to death has changed over the years from the very first experience to now. Did you become hard or callous, or did you treat it as clinical, or has it become just something in daily life, or how do you feel? Thank you."

Doctor: "I think it's very true to say that over the years, one certainly does become hardened to death. It's rather like one's first operation where most people seem to faint on the floor. You obviously have to become hardened to it in the sense that you can steel yourself and can cope with it mentally. But nevertheless, the shock of death, the suddenness of it sometimes, the unexpected nature of it is something that you can never completely reconcile. Continually, of course, in one's life it is an enemy. It comes perhaps to defeat what has been an otherwise successful operation or it comes to perhaps take away what has been otherwise a very good cure. And so as one naturally does become somewhat hardened to suffering and to death, it's inevitable. One's constant prayer, of a Christian doctor particularly, is that one might be kept sufficiently sensitive, that one can appreciate this fact and not become hard and callous."

David: "Well now, taking up this point that death is an enemy, the Bible says this too, but to you, your home calling is a fight against death. You're seeking to have the victory over it again and again, but you must know that ultimately you can't have a complete victory. You can postpone this enemy, but you can't put it off forever, which brings me to the question of is death always a bad thing in your experience? Sometimes we hear this phrase, 'A merciful release.' Someone who's suffering, someone who's in pain, someone who's gone through a lot; and one feels that death comes as a good thing then. Do you feel that sometimes death is a good thing in this sense?"

Doctor: "Accepting the fact, as you have already said, that everyone must die and that sooner or later the human body does become so frail and so diseased, death then is obviously a release, and one must accept it as such. Of course, it introduces many other problems, as to whether you should hasten it along when someone is obviously near the end. These problems, of course, are very difficult and have been subject to much recent controversy."

David: "Where would you draw the line? Some say that if the patient requests death they should be given death; if their relatives request it, the poor doctor is caught in this dilemma. Where would you draw the line?"

Doctor: "Well, it seems to me that the whole emphasis of one's training and one's upbringing and one's Hippocratic Oath is that one's job is to preserve life, and to frustrate death. Therefore, one should not adopt the role of an executioner. This, of course, involves other recent legislation that's gone through Parliament, about which many doctors are most unhappy. It seems to me that there's this dichotomy and one's going to become almost schizophrenic; half the time one is seeking to save life, preserve life, cure people, and on the other hand one is taking the power to terminate life. I think that one loses the confidence of one's patients, if they're not sure whether you're going to come along one day and stop treating them, but kill them. Similarly, within one's own mind the conflict is very hard. I think if people wish to have people to terminate life either in utero or at the end then they should train special people to do it. I think it's quite impossible."

David: "Now there was a doctor on the television this week who said that with someone who was completely helpless and hopeless, that if, for example, pneumonia set in, he would allow it to take its course rather than try to stop it.

Doctor: "This is very true, and I think there's a lot of difference between deliberately terminating life and frustrating, what one might call, the course of nature. If pneumonia develops in someone who's got severe inoperable disease or has had an operation which has obviously just not gone right and there's no real hope for a happy life for them, then I think to use the modern resources that we have to just prolong life is wrong. Similarly, if someone is perhaps going through severe pain one will give an injection which will relieve the pain, which at the same time one knows may well terminate life. This seems to be quite different to specifically, at someone's conscious request, terminating their life."

David: "I think we'd better just explain to the congregation what the Hippocratic Oath is. It sounded a little like hypocritical. I don't think many will realise that your fight against death is not based on a Christian principle, but on something else, so would you tell us a bit about Hippocrates?"

Doctor: "It's been a long time since I took the Hippocratic Oath and I must admit that I couldn't recite it to you or give you all the details of it, but basically it is that one's job is to go into the homes of patients and to treat them and to seek to cure them, in nursing, and always to frustrate against any crooked practice or any sense in which one is seeking to terminate life. This is all very much part and parcel of the Hippocratic Oath, which is, I suppose a humanitarian thing and which the Christian faith is added to."

David: "Dated when?"

Doctor: "About five hundred BC."

David: "So before Christ this oath was prepared for the medical profession. Now I'd like to ask you about one of the biggest questions that occurs to me and to relatives when somebody is, humanly speaking, incurable. Telling them is a very big issue and a delicate one. What do you feel about telling people that they're dying?"

Doctor: "I think that generally it's something that one ought to do. There are exceptions to this. Sometimes people do not want to know, and they make it quite clear by their attitude and how they speak. Other times, they are too ill to be told. Other times, quite honestly, they're just not perhaps intelligent enough to be able to assimilate the facts that you are going to give them.

But generally speaking, I think that for people to be told that the disease from which they are now suffering is something that they are not likely to recover from, although one may not be able to put a specific time to it, I think is a helpful thing. One of the most tragic things, I think, is the double block which one so often sees played with relatives and patients, where relatives think they're protecting the patient and the patient all along knows within his own heart the true facts of the case and he is deceiving relatives."

David: "Yes, I was going to say, you and I have both had experience of people who said, 'Don't tell them. They don't know,' and we've discovered very quickly that they did know and that there is an artificial atmosphere around. Who do you think should tell the person? Who is the best normally?"

Doctor: "Certainly, working in a hospital, I feel that very often we are not the right people. If it's going to be anyone in the medical profession, I think the practitioner who knows the patient and can perhaps choose the moment in their own home and in their own environment. Otherwise, ideally, I would think probably someone in the family, a relative. But I think this can be very hard and a lot depends on the relative."

David: "Very difficult, and there's a crucial moment when they can tell, and beyond that it's too late. Most people die peacefully — is that true or not?"

Doctor: "Yes, I would say so. I think there may be much suffering before death sometimes, but ultimately, in my experience this would be true, yes."

David: "I read in a book by a minister that he had never seen anyone die in any other way than peacefully, no matter what their life had been like, which raises the question: if everybody does die peacefully, what difference have you noticed between Christians dying and non-Christians dying? Have you noticed any?"

Doctor: "Yes, I think it's important to make the point. I think some Christians have the idea that only Christians know how to die. In one sense that may be right, but generally speaking, if we get the impression that all non-Christians shake and quiver and cower, this is quite wrong. I think that it is common for a Christian to die with a sort of quiet, tranquil hope. There's a peace about it as he realises, well, it's like having an anaesthetic before an operation and something that he's going to come through and wake up from. Whereas, so often, the non-Christian dies with a kind of stoic fortitude; he's hoping for the best, but if there isn't anything there, well it's blackout and that's it. I think this is the difference."

David: "How has all this affected your own thinking? You are a Christian. You've seen death quite often. Have you thought about your own death? This is a personal question. How has your own attitude been affected by your experience as a Christian doctor?"

Doctor: "I think it has been. Have I thought about my own death? I think probably no more than you or most people in the congregation. It's like illness. You see so much that you don't believe that it can happen to you, and often doctors are the very worst people. They present far later with their symptoms often than members of the public. As a Christian has it helped me? Yes, I think it has. To be with someone perhaps who's a very vital and live personality with whom one is conversing and then just suddenly, perhaps, through some complication that suddenly set in, they go, and there's just a body there. I find it just on the basis of human instinct, quite apart from Christian faith, impossible to believe that that personality has been snuffed out."

David: "So that your scientific training as a doctor hasn't, in that sense, ruled out your belief in life after death? The biologist who dissected a body and said he didn't find a soul anywhere in it, what is your reaction to that?"

Doctor: "Well, I think there are many abstract features to life which you'll not find by dissection, but there's no doubt you wouldn't find the human personality. But on the other hand, the human personality is a very real thing. Sorry, I think probably that one's scientific knowledge in a sense is strengthened by one's faith rather than the other way around."

David: "Well, thank you very much indeed for coming along and talking with us this morning."

....

I am sure you know the story—because it is so famous now—of when the first Christian missionaries came to Northumbria, which is my home territory up in the north of England. The missionaries arrived at the court of King Edwin and he invited them to a banquet. I want you to imagine the scene. It was a long, low hall with a doorway at one end and a doorway at the other end, a rush floor, and then lamps around the walls. The king entertained these missionaries and asked them many questions about their religion, which was new to him. As he talked, a sparrow flew in one door, through the lighted room and out of the other door. King Edwin turned to the missionaries and said, "My life is like that. I come out of the unknown; I pass through the lighted room of this world; I go out into the darkness. Can your religion tell me anything about that? Where do I go?" They were able to tell him, and King Edwin became a Christian, and Northumberland became a Christian territory.

The question that Job asked way back in the Old Testament is still the biggest question: "If a man dies, shall he live again?" What we are interested in is not whether I live on in other people's memories, or whether I live on in the work I have done, or in my children, or in the influence I have been, but whether I live on as a person. "If a man dies, shall he live again?" and that is the question that we are going to look at in this book. Let us first of all look at the fact of death, and having looked at it very squarely, we shall move on. But it is vital that we should face up to the fact of death.

The poets are unanimously sure of the fact. Here are just two. "One thing is certain, and the rest is lies; / The flower that once has blown forever dies." Or another poem: "Death lays his icy hand on kings: / Sceptre and Crown / Must tumble down, / And in the dust be equal made / With the poor crookèd scythe and spade." There is one death every second, somewhere.

Every time we go on the roads we face death. It can come suddenly or slowly, unexpectedly or expected. It comes to old and it comes to young. There has never been unemployment or strikes in the undertaking profession, and I think there never will be to the end of history. Now if a fact is as certain as this, how utterly foolish it is for someone never to prepare for it. Supposing you knew that you were going to Canada in six months' time, going to live there permanently. You would be an utter fool if you never thought about it, if you never read about Canada, if you never prepared, if you never asked what you should take and what you should leave behind. If you never made some preparation for the journey you would be an utter fool. It would catch you unprepared; you would not be ready for it. Yet the simple fact is that millions of people, knowing absolutely certainly that they are going to die, don't want to hear about it, don't want to think about it, don't ever try to get ready and never ask the question, "What can I take and what must I leave behind?"

Here are just a few more verses again from the Old Testament: "The day one dies is better than the day he is born. It is better to spend your time at funerals than at festivals, for you are going to die, and it is a good thing to think about it while there is still time. Sorrow is better than laughter, for sadness has a refining influence upon us. A wise man thinks much of death while the fool thinks only of having a good time now." Now, that divides the world into the wise people who think about death and the foolish people who put it out of their minds.

Now lest somebody think that is Old Testament stuff, let me remind you that the only man Jesus ever called a fool was the man who never thought about death and who didn't make provision for it—a man who said, "I'm going to build up my business, pull down my barns and build greater." God said to him, "Thou fool. This night thy soul shall be required of thee. You're going to have to leave it all behind and you've never thought about this. You've never prepared for it."

A man lived not far from where we lived in Buckinghamshire, and when he came to the end of the road he had a strong faith. They told him, and he wrote to his immediate relatives and he invited them to come and stay. This was what he wrote in the letter: "Come and see how a Christian dies." That is an amazing challenge. A man who had been prepared for this for years; a man who had been thinking about it; a man who was ready for it; a man who was journeying on and he was now about to say goodbye.

There is an extreme reluctance in our day to face up to this greatest fact of life. It shows in many ways, but in recent decades, mourning has been frowned upon. It is now considered not the "done" thing to mourn. You mustn't let people know you have been bereaved. You mustn't wear black. You mustn't make the funeral procession go slowly. You must get it all over with quickly, and this has been a striking change over the last fifty years in British society. I remember talking with a sociologist, a man in his fifties, who had spent two years studying the British attitude to death. He had interviewed thousands of bereaved people. He had studied our social practice, and he had come to the conclusion that Britain today is on the run from death.

You mustn't even use the word "died" about someone. You can use "pass away", but not "died". You must not state the fact. You must dress it up in other language in such a way that people don't realise. No more do we have novels being widely read with such deathbed scenes as that of Little Nell in *The Old Curiosity Shop*. That kind of Victorian melodrama is out. While there is a preoccupation with violent death in the entertainment world and in novels, the stark fact of death is evaded. People are running away from it; even in church is this true. About eighty years ago, you would hear preachers regularly mention death. Now you rarely hear a sermon on death itself.

Two men were talking, one of whom was a Christian and the other was not. The one who was not said, "Now you've faced death," and the Christian said, "Yes." "You believe you're going to survive death?" "Yes," said the Christian. "You believe you'll go to heaven when you die?" said the non-believer. The Christian said, "Yes, I do, but don't let's talk about anything so morbid," and revealed straight away that even as a Christian, as a churchgoer, he felt that talk of death and heaven was morbid. When you consider that our forefathers rejoiced that death was conquered and looked forward to heaven and talked about it constantly, you realise that the phobia, and it is a phobia, has gripped society and is creeping right into the church.

I'll give you another illustration. Take all the hymn books produced in recent decades and you will notice numerically, statistically, there are fewer and fewer hymns about heaven and life after death in every new hymn book. The number of hymns about heaven is going down, so we are on the run from this fact. Why? Why do people not like the subject? Why do we want to shut it out of our minds? Well, there are a number of reasons.

One is we are getting too comfortable here. Life is too good here to think of leaving it. We are getting so settled here that the thought of death says to us, "You're going to leave all this," and we have so much here to leave now that we are more reluctant to leave it. A church member was going around house-to-house visiting and came to someone's door and said, "We're coming around to invite you to come to our church. Our vicar is going to preach a special series of sermons on heaven and we'd like you to come and listen to him." One householder, looking around a lovely house with fitted carpets and everything money could buy, and swimming pool in the garden and a couple of cars in the garage, said, "Tell your vicar this is heaven." This would be a very honest reaction. Life is too good for us to think of leaving it. We have far more than our grandparents had. For them, they didn't have to leave so much. We have to leave so much more, which means that we don't want to be reminded that we're not here forever.

A very wealthy man put most of his money into pictures and he had those pictures hung all over his large home, each with a light over and all arrayed for visitors to see. One night his butler saw him going around and saw him with tears in his eyes. He was looking at his pictures and he was muttering to himself this: "You make it so hard to die. You make it so hard to die." This is why Jesus said two thousand years ago, "Invest in heaven; don't lay up treasure for yourselves on earth, because where your treasure is your heart will be locked up too. Lay up for yourselves treasure in heaven. If your heart is locked up there then it won't be a break when it comes."

A second reason is, of course, that people no longer believe in any world other than the world that you can touch and see and hear and taste and smell. In other words, there is a widespread disbelief in any other world besides this one, a material, tangible world that we know. Around thirty years ago, a journalist said, "Forty years ago, the British people stopped believing in hell. Twenty years ago, the British people stopped believing in heaven." I think he was probably largely right, although according to an independent television Gallup poll, only sixty-five per cent of the British people no longer believe in anything; any other world, any life after death. The other thirty-five per cent apparently still do.

A third reason is that we don't like any disturbing ideas, and death is only one of many ideas that does disturb us. A scene comes on the television showing children starving and perhaps you switch over to another channel to put this disturbing thought out of your mind. We live in a day in which there is such a desire to enjoy the present that anything at all that disturbs the present can be switched off. It may well be that that is why we are on the run from death.

A fourth reason, and a deep reason that has always applied, is that none of us likes to end a relationship. When we have formed a relationship, we don't like to end it. It is very interesting to notice that people adjust themselves to ending a relationship by death in exactly the same ways in which people adjust themselves to ending a holiday with a crowd they know they will never be with again. One way is to take a whole lot of photographs or exchange souvenirs. There are all kinds of ways of ending relationships. For example, after you haver been on a fortnight's holiday overseas with a tour party. The first day on the bus you didn't know each other. Halfway through the holiday you were on Christian name terms. By the end of the holiday, you were exchanging addresses and I don't know what else, but the relationships are going to end.

It is interesting that you will end the relationships of a holiday in the same way as you will tend to end them when death comes. You will either say, "Well, I'll just wash my hands of this whole party and just not think about them again. I'll just recall the memories and not even try to keep the relationship," or you will try to treasure some photograph of the party, some memento, but the same relationships will [not] be kept up in the same way. In other words, none of us likes to end relationships. But deep down, I would say that the reason why we are on the run from death is that most of us fear it.

Now let us look at this fear a little more closely. Cliff

Richard was once asked, "Do you fear death?" and he said an amazing thing and a very penetrating thing, which, as Christians, I think many of us would echo, and he is a Christian. He said, "I am not afraid of death, but I am afraid of dying." Now that was a very honest reply. He was not afraid of death. The fear of death had been conquered for him by Christ, but he was afraid of dying. Now why should people be afraid of dying, who are not afraid of death?

Well, one reason is the weakness that can precede it and lead up to it, whether physical or mental. I confess to you quite freely that after I have visited some elderly people who in extreme physical and often mental weakness have to be cared for like little children, I find myself echoing the Reverend John Wesley's prayer when he said, "Lord, let me not live to be useless." I think most of us would say that. Not all of us will have that privilege. It is wonderful to die in the harness, but I think many of us are afraid of dying because of the weakness that comes before it, and linked with that because of the suffering that can come before it. I think most of us have that apprehension of prolonged suffering. But that is not in a sense dying; that is what goes before it.

Why should we be apprehensive of dying itself? Many people are. One reason is, of course, that it is a new experience which we have never had before, and I think most of us are nervous of something we have never been through before. That is when nerves come in. If you have been baptised, I am sure you were nervous before you were baptised. Now knowing what is involved, I am sure you would not be nervous again. In a sense, you probably wish you could be baptised again without your nervousness, because it wasn't necessary. But you were nervous because it was a new experience. You had not been baptised before. In the same way, death or dying is a new experience which we have not had before.

It is also a lonely experience at a human level, in that it is an experience that we must pass through alone, by ourselves. This is where we need Jesus Christ, because your relatives can't go with you, but Jesus can and does. I gained so much evidence of this while visiting people in hospital. I have noticed that a Christian dying does not have a lonely experience during that time, because Jesus Christ can go right through it with them. It is a final experience, and this is perhaps where the fear begins to come in. We must face it very squarely. It is a reminder that your life is over, that the time of decision has gone, that the time of sowing is now behind you.

I don't think there is anyone reading this who could face the end of life and say, "I can face it without any regrets, without any twinges of conscience so that if I could live my life over again, I would not have done this differently and made that decision in another way." Every one of us when we come to the end of our life will have regrets about how we have lived it. The time of sowing is over. The time of decision is over. Our life has been lived and we can't have it again. We fear the challenge of being faced with a completed life.

But the other side of it is this. Just suppose that now the time of sowing is over; there is a time of reaping. Just suppose that now I have played the fool there is a bill to be paid. Just suppose that the Bible is right and that deep down the instinct of the human heart that in the next world justice does apply if it doesn't in this, then I think we begin to touch the deepest spring of the fear of death. In other words, the real question is this: if there is nothing after death, then people could face it without fear. They might dislike it, they might postpone it as long as possible, but when it came, they could face it. I have noticed this, that people who do not believe there is anything after death are not afraid of death. It is the possibility of something lying beyond that brings the fear.

LIFE AFTER DEATH

John Wesley was in a cart, going to Hyde Park Corner, Tyburn as it was then, with a man about to be hanged. The man who was going to be hanged was trembling, and John Wesley said, "Are you afraid?" He said, "Yes, I'm afraid." "What are you afraid of? Are you afraid to die?" "No, I'm not afraid to die. I've faced death a hundred times." He had been a highwayman. John Wesley said, "What are you afraid of then?" He replied, "I'm afraid of what lies beyond." The fear of death was the fear of facing up to his life—the fear that he was going to be called to account. Therefore, we are going to face the future, life after death, in these chapters.

There are almost as many ideas about life after death as there are people. Some of those ideas are terribly mistaken. I want now to give you six that I have come across. First of all, there is the idea around that death is not real, that it doesn't actually happen, that it is only something in the mind. That is an unusual idea. Not many people hold it. This is one of the ideas that is related to the basic philosophy and outlook of Christian Science—that death is unreal. It doesn't really happen. It is only in your mind.

Secondly, there is the idea I have mentioned already that the way you live on is in your children, in their memory, in the work you have done. There is a Chinese proverb that there are only four things worth doing in life—planting a tree, writing a book, building a house and having a son; the reason being that these are the only four things that live on after you have gone and will cause people to remember you. That is a false idea that that is how you live on.

Thirdly, there is the idea I have already mentioned that when death comes that is the end, nothing more for you—that's curtains, that's lights, that's oblivion—nothing at all, just nothing. Now that is utterly mistaken according to the Bible. By the way, those who believe this tend to go on to say that heaven and hell are what you make of your life here, and that, in fact, people live in heaven or hell here. That again is an utterly false idea. Nobody in this world is living in heaven or hell. You can't make your own heaven or hell.

Fourthly, there is the idea of reincarnation, that after I have died, I will come back as someone else. Now I lived in digs for a time with two dear ladies who were quite convinced that I was what they called "an old soul". I didn't understand this term technically for some time. But I later came to realise what they meant, that I had a previous existence. The only difficulty with this idea was that I had no recollection of it whatsoever, and therefore it was of no use to me. But this idea of reincarnation is a very widespread idea, more in the East than the West, but people in the West are beginning to believe it now. Even Christian ministers are toying with the idea in some cases. Now that idea, you know, be kind to your four-footed friends, a duck may be somebody's mother, is an idea that you will find nowhere in the Bible. That, by the way, is the extreme of reincarnation that if you have misbehaved you will come back as an animal and not as a human being.

A fifth idea is that when you die you are finished with your body forever and your soul goes floating on into some lovely existence, and that is the total truth about the future. That is not true either. Your body is not finished with, as we'll see. Then there is the idea which we call universalism, which is that that everybody believes, when they die they will go to a better place. Somebody walked around a cemetery once and read all the grave stones and then commented to one of the men working in the cemetery, "Where do you bury all the sinners in this place?" because he saw nothing but everybody is good, everybody has gone to the right place, everybody is happy and so on. Well, that is not a biblical idea, and sometimes when I have seen the phrase, "Rest in Peace", and known something of the name or the person whose name is above those words, I have wondered if that phrase isn't a very long way from the truth.

How are we to know? Some people say, "You can't know; there's no way of knowing. Your guess is as good as mine and we're all in the dark, so if you like to believe this, that's fine. I like to believe that, leave me alone." Well, science can't tell us because science can only deal with this world. Sentiment can't tell us, but it is the most dangerous guide in the matter of life after death. Sentiment begins its creed by saying, "I like to feel that," and then adds whatever is enjoyed in feeling: "I like to feel that he's doing this," or "she's doing that."

No, the real source of our knowledge must not be science or sentiment, it must be scripture. If we believe that this book is not just a book written by human beings, but a book of God giving the mind of God, then the one person in the universe who knows what happens when I die is God. Let me give you certain statements which I am going to enlarge upon in subsequent chapters that give you in summary form what the Bible says about death.

Here they are. First, death is real. The Bible takes the idea of death utterly seriously. It is not afraid to use the word "died" and the word "death" frequently, and if you go through and underline these words in your Bible, you will be astonished. Death is real. It is faced squarely. The cross is the heart of our faith. Therefore, the Christian faith is built upon a faith that has looked death in its most violent form in the face — death in its most horrible aspect, of a young man of thirty-three murdered. We have looked at death squarely at the heart of our faith and come through it, so that the first thing about the biblical attitude to death is this — death is real.

Secondly, according to my Bible, death is an enemy. It is an alien. It is a hostile intrusion into the world. It is therefore to be fought in the name of God. It is therefore something that belongs not to God's order, but to Satan's order. It is something that need never have happened to men and women. It is something that is tied up with evil, so those who say death is a good thing are saying the opposite of the Bible. The Bible always says death is real and it is a bad thing. It is an evil thing. It is an enemy. It is a robber, and it is something we must fight.

Thirdly, the Bible states that death is never the end of a single person. It may be the separation of the body and the spirit, but it is neither the end of the spirit nor of the body. It is never the end. To take only one saying of Jesus to prove this, Jesus teaches us that all who are in the grave shall come forth—all. There is no qualification at all; death is never the end for a single person.

Fourthly, the Bible states that beyond death there lies not one destiny, but two and only two. There is unequivocal teaching in the Bible about this. We are not all going to the same place. We are going to one of two places.

Fifthly, this life is decisive for which of those two destinies is ours, meaning that what we do here before death is absolutely decisive for what we shall be doing after death.

Sixthly, therefore, death is always followed, although not immediately, by judgment. By that I mean the day of reckoning, the day of accounting. The New Testament states it as simply as this: "It is appointed to a man once to die," that is all, once, "and after that, the judgment."

Seventhly, following from that, the sting of death is sin. Now what do we mean by that? The thing that makes death so horrible is the fact that we will not have lived as we should have lived before we died. That is the real thing that makes it difficult to face. That is the real problem that confronts us when we confront the fact that after death we shall be in a condition that has been decided before death. It is sin; it is wrongdoing that makes it so difficult. Behind all our other fears of a lonely experience and a new experience, pain, weakness, suffering, behind all those fears is deep down in the human heart the fear that after death I pay for what I did before death.

Lastly in this chapter, death in the Bible is a conquered enemy. Why? Because sin has been conquered; when Christ died, sin was conquered and the sting taken out of death. When Christ rose again, death itself was conquered and it is for this reason that Jesus did use a euphemism for death. He used to use the phrase, "fallen asleep"—so and so "has fallen asleep". This is a lovely phrase. "Passed away" is not a Christian phrase to use, because in the Bible "passed away" means utterly finished. "The world passes away; prophecy passes away," meaning it is utterly finished, so don't say passed away. That means utterly finished. Say fallen asleep, because if you say fallen asleep, you mean that person is in a condition that they can be aroused and woken up from.

So, when Jairus's daughter was reported dead, you remember that Jesus said, "She is not dead. She is sleeping," meaning that he was going to wake her up, which he did. When Lazarus died, Jesus told his disciples, "Lazarus is sleeping." They thought, "Well that's all right. He's just in healthy sleep after his fever," but Jesus said, "No, I didn't mean that—to you, Lazarus is dead; to me, he's asleep. I'm going to wake him up." Catherine Marshall, the wife of Peter Marshall, the United States Senate chaplain, in that lovely book *A Man Called Peter*, the story of her husband, describes how he was taken away desperately ill from the home one morning, quite young, and how she said goodbye to him. She felt in her heart that she would not see him again and she didn't. His last words to her were these: "I'll see you in the morning. I'll see you in the morning."

Christians speak of those who have fallen asleep in Christ Jesus—sin has been conquered, death has been conquered and therefore we can say, "They're only asleep. They haven't passed away. They're asleep and they will be woken up." I'll come on to more of that in the next chapter when discussing the condition of those who have died and who await with us the resurrection morning. What happens between death and resurrection? What does the Bible tell us?

But let us rejoice now that of all the people in the universe, Christians can look death squarely in the face, without fear, and know that it is an enemy, but a conquered enemy. Remember the words of Winston Churchill about the late King George VI, who was certainly a Christian. Winston Churchill said about the late king, "During the last few months the king has walked with death as if it were a companion, an acquaintance whom he recognised and did not fear. During the last few months, the king has been sustained, not only by his natural buoyancy of spirit, but by the sincerity of his Christian faith." May God grant us all the same.

Chapter 2

Between Death and Resurrection

Read Luke 16:19–31, a passage in which Jesus said more about life after death than anywhere else in all his teaching. It is in the form of a story, or a parable, but it is true to life and the afterlife.

What exactly happens to a person when they die? Certain physical processes stop almost immediately—breathing stops, the heartbeat stops, circulation stops, and it is by the stopping of these things that we usually say, "This person has died." Other processes go on for quite a time, for example, the growth of hair continues for some time after death and a number of other bodily processes continue for some time. After a certain length of time, these processes also stop. Then decay and ultimately decomposition come to the human body. We all know this, however unwilling we are to face it.

This is what will happen to the body that I use to preach, but that is not an answer to the question, "What happens to a man when he dies?" I have only told you what happens to his body when he dies, and if a man is only a body then I have described the whole thing. He has ceased to be. You will never see or meet him again. If a man is only a body, only a physical creature, if all that I think and feel and do is the result of my physical glands and enzymes and hormones, then I have already answered the question, but the Bible is quite emphatic that a man is very much more than a body; indeed, that the body is almost a secondary part of him. The Bible describes the human body in terms of a tent in which the real person lives—a tabernacle. It also describes the body as a suit of clothes, worn by the real person, and so Paul, for example, talks very confidently and without fear of the day when he will no longer live in this tent or this suit of clothes, and so he is not disturbed.

I remember walking past a cemetery with a Christian man whose parents' bodies lay in the cemetery, and he said, "You know, I just think of their bodies as overcoats. They are not in there." In fact, once you can see that a cemetery is no more than a cloakroom, you are on your way to getting the right view towards death. A cemetery is a cloakroom where we put aside the old clothes that we have worn for whatever it has been—seventy, or by reason of strength, eighty years, and so the Bible really emphatically states that the real person is not the body, however intimately the body has been connected with the real person. The body is the tent, the suit of clothes which we put off one day when we will no longer live in it.

A dear old Christian was asked by a minister, "How are you?" and he replied, "Well, the roof leaks a bit, the walls are cracking, but I'm fine, I'm fine," and he was just stating what the New Testament states, what Paul stated: "My outward man is decaying, giving up, packing up, but my inward man is being renewed every day, getting stronger and better every day." That is growing old from the Christian point of view. The outside may decay and may get older and more tired; the inside should be getting stronger and better all the time, being renewed.

In this we are quite different from all animals, and therefore, death to the man is completely different from death to the animal. If man is simply the product of an evolutionary process, this would not be true. Man is a unique combination of the physical and the spiritual, the natural and the supernatural. The meaning of death for man, unlike the animals, is not annihilation. It is not oblivion. It is not the end of that man. What, then, happens to a man when he dies?

The answer is an answer that no doctor or scientist could give you. The answer is, when a man dies, it is the moment of separation between his body and his spirit. That is what we understand by death—the moment when two things that have been intimately linked together, so close that you can't think of them apart, having never known them apart; they spring apart and become two separate things.

This, then, is the meaning of death, and it is very interesting that even in popular speech people recognise this. Somebody once said to me, "Oh, it is hard keeping body and soul together these days." Now what did she mean? She meant precisely what she said. Keeping those two parts together is life. Death is when they separate, and so living is keeping body and soul together. Take another saying—people talk about not giving up the ghost yet. What do they mean? They mean precisely the same thing. Don't so accept death that you allow your spirit to escape your body now. The very dot-dot-dot, dash-dash-dash, dot-dot-dot—SOS, is precisely keep our souls and our bodies; keep them together; save our souls, even though it is the body that is in peril.

Now the Bible puts it as simply as that and this is what, for example, the book of Ecclesiastes says about death, defining it: "Then shall the dust return to the earth as it was and the spirit shall return to the God who gave it." Death is separation between these two things. We know what happens to the body. It came from the dust of the earth. There is not a particle in my body that cannot be found in the crust of the earth somewhere, and it goes back to that—it came from that: "Dust thou art, and unto dust shalt thou return." If you rub your hands together and go on rubbing, you can produce on a sheet of white paper a little pile of grey dust, the dead cells of your skin. You can look at that dust and say, "That is a little bit of my body going back to where it came from." That is what happened to the body. We know that, but the question I am concerned with now is, "What happens to the spirit?"

James, in the New Testament, lest you think that I am entirely relying on Old Testament teaching in this chapter, says, "The body without the spirit is dead." In other words, that is precisely what constitutes death. The body is now without the spirit. The two have been separated and are apart. I think it is very interesting that when Jesus died, he virtually told us the same thing. His body was near the end of its earthly life after thirty-three years and hours of torture. What did he say to God in the last moment of his life? He did not say, "Into thy hands I commit myself," or "Into thy hands I commit my body." His body would have to be looked after by others. He said, "Into thy hands I commit my spirit," and having said this, he gave up the spirit or the ghost. The spiritual part of him he gave to God. Joseph of Arimathea had to look after the physical part; there was the separation of the two.

This idea fits in very well with modern philosophy and with the ancient Greek philosophy, which was the main kind of thinking in our Lord's day. Those who do believe in life after death accept this general framework, that whatever else it includes it cannot include this body. This body must be left behind. If there is a life after death, it must be because the spiritual part of man survives. Now, that fits in with ordinary thinking until the New Testament makes a startling statement, and it is this: that that is not the final condition of a person. It is only a temporary separation; that in fact, there is coming a day when body and soul come together again.

This is what is meant by the word "resurrection", which only Christians use. The Greeks, if they had stood to recite their creed would have said, "I believe in the immortality of the soul, this spiritual part going on forever," but the Christians, when they stood up and said what they believed, said, "I believe in the resurrection of the body." In other words, at some future point after the separation of body and soul, the two come together again. That is what we mean by resurrection, and we believe it. Why do we believe it?

Well, first of all, because Jesus actually did this for a handful of people. He brought body and soul together again. In some cases, this was a few hours after death; in one case, it was four days after death, but he proved that he had the power to bring body and soul back into relationship with each other even after the body had been subject to decay and disintegration. Do you remember Martha's practical words when Jesus said, "Open that grave"? In the climate of the Middle East, she was perfectly right to say, "It just isn't fit to open by this time." She said it in more direct language than that, and Jesus said, "Open the tomb. I am the resurrection and the life. I have the power to bring body and soul together, even after corruption has set in."

We supremely believe in this possibility of body and soul being reunited again because of Easter; because Jesus himself was reunited three days and three nights after he had said, "I commit my spirit into your hands." Three days and three nights after his body had been put back in the earth from which it came, body and spirit were reunited. This is the heart of our Christian faith, and even some Christians find it difficult to believe. The world finds it impossible. When he came back from the dead, Jesus said, "Look, I am not a spirit—not any longer." He had been a spirit for three days and three nights, but he said emphatically after his resurrection, "I am not a spirit, for a spirit does not have flesh and bones such as you see I have. Come and touch me." He invited them to do this in order to prove that he was no longer a spirit, so that the biggest difference between a Christian and others is that the former thinks about life after death—if others do believe in life after death, they believe that we survive eternally as spirits.

Christians believe that there is coming a day when we will no longer be spirits, but once again embodied people, people that have flesh and bones with which they can express themselves. That makes heaven terribly real. That makes heaven a place, incidentally, which is why Jesus called it a place and not a state of the soul. That is why Archbishop William Temple once said, "Christianity is the most materialistic of all the world religions." It believes in the resurrection of the body, the redemption of our bodies, for which we all wait. In other words, when God saves a person, he doesn't just save their spirit. One day he will save their body too, the whole of them and make the whole of them what he intended them to be.

Now I come to the main subject, which may seem a rather long way around to it, but the point that you will have already grasped is this: for Jesus Christ himself and for us, there is an interval between death and resurrection. Between the separation of body and spirit and their coming together again, there is an interval. Long or short, there is an interval during which we will be disembodied spirits as Jesus was. The big question arises, "What will it be like? What will happen to us in the interval? Will we be unconscious or awake? Where will we be? What will we be doing?" I want to tackle such questions in this chapter.

The interval for our Lord was three days and three nights—not a very long interval, but an interval nonetheless. Christians have always been quite sure that it would be a mistake to say that he was in heaven. One of the phrases in the Apostles' Creed, which most Christians have accepted and used as a fair summary of biblical teaching, says, "He descended into Hades." By the way, the word "hell" was an English alteration, and it should never have got in. It is one of the most misleading things that could be said.

"He suffered under Pontius Pilate, was crucified, died and

was buried. He descended into Hades." The word "Hades" is not the word hell and should not be confused with it. It is not necessarily a bad word or a bad place or a bad state. It is a word that simply means the realm of departed spirits. It means wherever departed spirits are and whatever they are doing. That is what the Bible refers to, in the New Testament, in the Greek language, as Hades; but in the Old Testament, in the Hebrew language, Sheol. If you read the Revised Standard Version of the Bible, which is I think the best we have available, you will find that throughout the Old Testament, Sheol is the word used, and in the New Testament, Hades, for the interval between death and resurrection.

And so, the Apostles' Creed states, "He suffered under Pontius Pilate, was crucified, died, and was buried. He descended into Hades. On the third day he rose again, [body and spirit reunited] and he ascended into heaven." The word "heaven" is kept for the bodily resurrected person. I think it would clarify a lot of our thinking if Christians also kept the word heaven for after the resurrection when we shall have bodies and live in the place that he has prepared for us. But now let us come back to Hades. Are there any hints as to what it is like and what was happening in Hades when Jesus went there? He died; he became a disembodied spirit for three days and three nights.

The first clue lies in something he said to a dying thief who said, "Lord, remember me in that future day when you get to your kingdom." He was obviously thinking of heaven. He was thinking of a day way in the future and he believed that Jesus was the Christ and can get people into the kingdom of heaven at the end of history. He said, "Lord, when that happens, could you get me? Could you take me with you into it? Could you remember me?" Our Lord said that he would do more than that—he would promise him something that day.

Now you see what a wonderful reply it was. "Lord, when you come into your kingdom in the distant future, whenever it is, could I be in it?" Jesus said, "Today, I can comfort you with something right now." This means, of course, that you don't need to limit the comfort that is given to Christians when they die to things that are in the distant future. You can say some things about the interval, which are enough to make them look forward to it. What Jesus said to the dying thief was "Today we shall be together in paradise." He didn't use the word heaven, and our Lord was always careful in his use of words, lest he cause misunderstanding. Every word our Lord used counts, and he deliberately used the word paradise.

Now that is a very interesting word. It is a Persian word. It means essentially a garden and it means particularly a king's garden. Think of the garden outside Buckingham Palace, with that high wall around it, which you may or may not have been in. I haven't, and I don't suppose you have. You may have seen it from the top of a bus, and that may be the nearest most of us get to it, but there it is. That is Her Majesty's paradise. That is what the word means. It is her private garden. Anyone can go into it who is invited by the Queen, but you must wait for that invitation. If you walk with her in her garden it is by her invitation, her grace and favour. Paradise in the Bible, which, incidentally, is the word that is also used of the garden of Eden and pops up again at the end of the Bible in connection with the garden city, refers to the King's garden.

Now you notice that the garden is not the palace. The garden is not the Father's house. The garden is not a place of rooms. When our Lord talked about his Father's house and many rooms, he was quite clearly referring not to the interval after death, but to the distant future, because he said that he would come again and then you would be able to come with him to his Father's house. But what he is saying to the thief is that if he could not take him now into his Father's house, he could take him into the King's garden, and walk with him in the garden. They would be together there.

That is one clue that begins to tell us that, in a sense, the interval is much nearer to the kingdom than we can be here. As it were, one could almost describe the three stages like this: stage number one is to be on the top of a bus going through London and catching a glimpse of Buckingham Palace in the distance. That is the life we enjoy here. Stage number two is to get inside the garden, nearer still and walk with the King. Stage number three is to get right inside the palace itself, into the room reserved for you as a believer. If you think of it like that, you will realise that paradise will be very much better than anything we have had here, especially because we shall be walking in such close fellowship with the King.

In the olden days, and still today in some areas, a palace not only had a private garden where the king could walk with his friends, a palace also had a dungeon, a cell, which was not part of the palace itself. It was a prison, and it is very interesting that there are hints, also more than hints in the New Testament, that in the interval there is not only a garden, but a prison. One of the most extraordinary statements made, which is there in the Bible and on which the Apostles' Creed builds, is a statement by Peter, the big fisherman, to the effect that when Jesus died, he was dead in the flesh but alive in the spirit, and went and preached to the spirits in prison. We are told which ones in particular to whom he went and preached, which is very important.

He went and preached to the spirits of those who had been drowned in the Flood of Noah. Those who deny the historicity of the Flood of Noah are left with a problem here, because these are the people to whom Jesus went and preached between his death and resurrection. You notice they are said to be in prison, not in the garden. There is this other place. I will come back to this strange statement in a moment, but can you sense already that the Bible is saying that even though heaven and hell are not entered at death, after resurrection and in the future, there is already in the interval a distinguishing between two conditions—conditions of spirits rather than bodies, and one condition is likened to a garden and the other is likened to a prison, and both belong to the King.

It is this picture on which the rest of the New Testament seems to build. It is a picture, and we must accept it as a picture. We cannot begin to imagine what either is like in detail or in fact, but if you think of a prison and if you think of a garden, you are getting the right feel of it. Let us take the prison first, because I always prefer to get that out of the way first and then go on to the garden and finish up on a happy note. Very little is said about the prison. It will be a place of segregation. That is what going to prison means. It is not the prison diet, or anything that happens there. It is that you are shut off, shut out. That is the meaning of prison.

Judas will be there. It is said that when Judas hanged himself, he went to his own place, and this is clearly the place. Some of the angels will be there and, indeed, we are told twice in the New Testament that God has already put some of the angels in custody until the day of the great trial of both angels and men. There will be many other people there. I think the second thief will be there. The first thief will be in the garden, but I think the second will be there, so that while it is a place of segregation that doesn't mean there won't be plenty of people there.

It does mean that it will be segregation from God and from God's people, and whether we understand it or not, that is the worst kind of segregation there can ever be. Some people in this world are perfectly happy to live without God and to get as far from God's people as they can. They don't like

Christians and they don't like the Christ whom the Christians worship. Well, quite frankly, they will get their dearest wish immediately after they die, but they will begin to realise just how much they will miss both. There is also suffering, and it would be wrong of me if I didn't say this. What it is, I do not know. It will be mental suffering because in the story I read earlier, our Lord clearly indicates that memory will still be active and regret will be one of the most awful things to bear. There will be the regret of knowing that your life is over, that death has sealed your decisions, that your future course is set, and that there is really no altering it now.

Three things can be said about the prison, all of which are definite. First, those who are in it cannot go back from that prison to life itself. Our Lord clearly said this. The second thing we can say definitely is that they cannot go forward to the garden. They are in custody, awaiting appearance at court and there is no bail. Thirdly, they must go forward from that to something else. This is not a permanent condition. It is the interval of waiting.

Now I turn to paradise and here we find some lovely things. It is not the palace, but the park surrounding the palace. That is how we are to think of it—a step nearer to our heavenly home, much nearer. There are certain things about this garden which are lovely. Let me say straight away that in the interval we need not worry about the question where. Being disembodied spirits, spatial relationships, places, don't apply. So, to ask where they are is to ask a question that cannot be answered. When we get to the third stage, we can begin to talk of a place ("I go to prepare a place"), but we are not to think of the garden or the prison as necessarily a spatial place. Disembodied spirits don't need a place. We are talking about states.

Secondly, I am not sure that we are greatly helped by asking the question, "What is it like?" any more than by asking, "Where is it?" But there is one question I find a lot of people are troubled about and that is whether they are going to be awake or instead in a kind of Rip Van Winkle state, asleep over the centuries. It is interesting that his first name is on so many tombstones. Are we in a state of sleeping and unconsciousness for centuries and then wake up, so that, in fact, after the moment we die the next thing we know is waking up at resurrection, or are we in fact conscious?

There is no doubt about it that the New Testament has a number of passages in which the dead are said to have fallen asleep in the Lord. This is a phrase that is used a number of times, but the point I want to make is this. Souls, spirits, cannot sleep. Sleep is a physical function. Only bodies can sleep, and therefore the phrase fallen asleep I am quite sure refers to the appearance of the body. Physically a person is asleep when they are dead. It is their appearance. It is a very good word to describe their condition. It also carries the possibility of the body being woken up, but I think we are on very thin ice if we start applying the word sleep to spirits as well as to bodies and believe in what is called soul sleep. The Seventh-day Adventists believe this and so do a number of other cults, but I can't see it justified.

On the contrary, Paul says, "Whether we wake or sleep, we live with him." I don't think Paul would have said that if it were unconscious. The real question about the interval is not where it is, not what it is, but who it is with. The glorious thing to which Christians look forward here is that we shall be with Christ. If I am unconscious, that doesn't attract me one bit. I would say that would be a good deal worse than being here, because here I can be conscious and speak to Christ. No one would ever say, "I long to depart and be with Christ," if they were looking forward to centuries of unconscious fellowship.

It is quite clear that the emphasis of the New Testament is on conscious fellowship and the spirit can be conscious apart from the body. Paul says at one point that he knew "a man in Christ" who was "caught up to the third heaven". One day he went to heaven. During his lifetime he went to heaven, paid a visit. Paul says this: "Whether it was in the body or out of the body, I do not know". The point he is making is, you can be conscious out of the body. Indeed, you are, and so I believe that we look forward to conscious fellowship with Christ. Only with Christ? No, much more—with all Christ's people, whether they lived before or after his day. His people—we shall be with them.

We shall be with Abraham. Did you ever realise that Abraham was a Christian? He is. "Abraham rejoiced to see my day," said Jesus, "and he was glad," and a man who rejoices to see Jesus' day is a Christian. When Lazarus, that beggar, died he found himself sitting next to Abraham in the garden. We shall meet Abraham, and Isaac, and Jacob, and all of the men of faith of the Old Testament and all the people of faith since the New Testament. We shall be with Christians, with Christ's people. It is the King's garden party.

The third thing is we shall be with angels. I know this, that whether you go to the prison or the garden, you will believe in angels the first five minutes after you die even if you have never believed in them before. You will meet them, and one of the loveliest thoughts to me is that even if you die alone, unwanted, uncared for with nobody there to help you, God has angels waiting just the other side to care for you. His servants, the palace staff, are waiting in the garden. Lazarus died; he didn't even have a funeral. He was a beggar. Nobody cared for him, and the angels took him to Abraham.

We shall be with Christ. We shall be with Christians. We shall be with the angels. It is no wonder that even though Paul knew that he was going to be unclothed for the interval, disembodied, without flesh and bones, he preferred to be away from the body and at home with the Lord. That is why, when he faced certain death, although part of him wanted to stay and help, he longed to depart and be with Christ. It is paradise to the Christian. A great saint was asked this question: "What do you most look forward to as a Christian?" After a moment's thought he said, "The first five minutes after death." He had understood his Bible. He knew the truth, and he honestly meant just that.

I am now going to answer in brief six questions that I have been asked over the years about the interval between death and resurrection.

The first question: what decides whether we go to prison or paradise in the interval? I shall address the issue of judgment in chapter 4, and the answer is really that the same thing that decides your ultimate destiny decides the intermediate destiny. In a sentence, those who have never heard of Christ will be judged as to whether they have lived up to the light they have received through conscience, creation and other ways. Those who have heard of Christ will be judged by their response to him. Both these things happen in this life rather than in the interval, and, in fact, what we do in this life decides not only the third stage, but the second. Chapter 4 will give a full answer to that one.

Second question: is there a second chance? Now this is a question that many people ask. More and more people today believe that there is. May I say that the only hint I can find in the Bible anywhere for a second chance for anyone is the passage in Peter about those who were prematurely judged and drowned in the days of Noah. For the rest, the evidence in the scripture is overwhelmingly against any possibility of a second chance. There is a great gulf fixed and death would seem to be the end of choosing. It is a thing that one dare not gamble with or risk.

Third question: what about purgatory? Now the Roman Catholics have added a number of details, or compartments if you like, to the interval between death and resurrection. For example, they have taught about such places as *Limbus Infantum*, Limbo for short, where un-baptised babies go and various other things. One of the places they do believe in is purgatory. In their teaching, this place has two purposes—first, it is a place where we pay for our own sins unless they have been forgiven here. Therefore, it is a place of punishment. Secondly, it is a place of purging or cleansing, where those who die before they are saintly enough to enter heaven may gradually be put into a condition to do so.

In other words, there are two sorts of saints who die—saints who are perfect and ready for heaven, and they are canonised and called Saint so-and-so—and those who are not ready, which means most of us who must go to this further school as it were, those who believe in Jesus but are not yet saintly enough to live in heaven itself. It is because of this belief in purgatory that certain other practices and beliefs get such a grip on people who believe in it, practices and beliefs such as masses for the dead, indulgences, penance, and so on. They are all related to this one belief in purgatory. I can only state that nowhere in the entire Bible can I find a single trace of the idea of purgatory.

Indeed, there are three reasons why in fact it seems to me impossible that there should be such a place. First, Jesus was punished for all my sins. Why then, have I to be? That seems to me conclusive. Second, when I die physically, that will set me free from this body of sin and death. I am finished with sin; I am finished with Satan; I am finished with temptation. You cannot tempt a corpse, and it is through this body of sin and flesh that Satan gets hold of me one way or another, whether it is the lust of the eyes, the lust of the flesh or the pride of life. It is all connected with life in this body. Thirdly, if my physical death sets me free from all sin, when Christ comes again, I know I will be like him, for I shall see him as he is. I shall be like him and therefore there is no need for this school of cleansing. Therefore, starting from the Bible I cannot accept the idea of purgatory at all.

Fourth question: is it all right to pray for the dead? Now this is a very real issue today because a few decades ago, the Church of England brought out a service in which prayers for the dead were included. Increasingly, it is becoming common practice to do this. The official order of service brought out jointly by Roman Catholics, Anglicans, and the Free Church Council included prayers for those who died in the two World Wars. Now what do we think about this? It is quite obvious that if you have been praying for someone for years and years you can't just stop. It is quite obvious that you go on thinking about people who have died and talking about them. It is quite obvious that since you share everything with the Lord, you will go on talking to him about those who have died in him.

There is nothing in scripture to suggest that we should not talk about those who have died in our prayers, but that is a very different thing from praying for them, because if somebody says, "I want to pray for someone who's died," my question will be, "What are you going to pray for them? What need do you think they have that your prayer will help?" When that question is answered we begin to realise that prayers for the dead are useless. If a person is not saved by the time they are dead, there is that great gulf fixed, and if they are saved, then it is an act of unbelief to ask Jesus to look after them. He has promised to do so and we can be absolutely confident that everything we would wish for our loved ones that is right and good Jesus is already giving to them. There is no need to ask him to do so.

He has promised to look after us completely from the moment we die and therefore prayers for the dead are rightly not practised by those who accept the Bible's promises. It is those who are unsure of life after death who will pray for the dead. There is no Bible example or exhortation to pray for the dead and it is remarkable to me that a book that is constantly telling us to pray for the living never once tells us to pray for the dead. There is only one mention of a prayer for the dead in a writing, and that is in the second book of Maccabees, which is in the Apocrypha, which is not in the Bible but which is, as you know, in the Roman Bible.

Fifth question: do the dead watch us and can they pray for us? While Hebrews 12 does talk about a great cloud of witnesses around us, it is a little ambiguous as to whether it means they are watching us or looking at Jesus. It is ambiguous as to whether it means we should draw inspiration from them or intercession. I would feel inclined, though I cannot be dogmatic, to say that they are there for our inspiration, rather than intercession. Once you believe that the dead pray for us, it is a short step to offering prayers *to* the dead, *to* the saints, not just *for* them. Rather, we are to believe in the communion of saints. Christ has two hands. With one hand he holds those of us who are on earth. With the other hand he holds those who have lived and died in his faith and fear. Our communion is through him, rather than direct, and when we have the communion service, we enjoy the communion of saints and mystic sweet communion with those whose rest is won.

Final question: can we communicate with the dead? In the next chapter, I am going to deal with spiritualism, but the answer in a nutshell is the Bible absolutely forbids God's people ever to attempt to try to communicate with the dead. In the next chapter, I will tell you why.

Chapter 3

Resurrection

Read 1 Corinthians 15:35–58

In these chapters, we are not only speaking about the Word of God, we are talking to people who have had to work this out in their daily life and think about it. In the present chapter, I am going to include a talk that I had with Mr Ennis Matthews some decades ago. He had been a member of the church of which I was pastor since 1938.

David: "Matt, you work as a physiotherapist. Could you sum that up in a few sentences. Tell us what it involves."

Matt: "Well, most of the people, I think, know my stock definition of this, but it's half way between an all-in wrestler and a vet. But physiotherapy as such means the healing of things by physical means, and that means that largely one is dealing with what you might call the mechanics of the body. Its construction, the way it's made, the way these things get out of order largely through muscles, joints, nerves, ligaments. Sometimes other bits as well; we deal with lungs and even digestive organs occasionally. But it's largely the mechanics of the body in which we deal. Unlike surgeons, who in these days particularly are able to put in new bits or at least part-used ones, shop-soiled a bit perhaps, we have to just patch up the bits that are left and make the best of what you've got."

David: "Even so, Matt, you must've come to some similar conclusions to the psalmist who said, 'I am fearfully and wonderfully made.' Have you come to the conclusion that the body is about the most wonderful machine on earth? Tell us some wonderful things that you've discovered about the body."

Matt: "Well, the body itself is simply a marvellous piece of machinery. For one thing, the way in which it is used—or, more accurately, abused—is something which you would never do to a piece of machinery at home. If we did the things to the motor cars and refrigerators for which we have guarantees nowadays, the same sort of treatment that we give our bodies, I don't think any maker would ever say that he was bound by the guarantee that he gave. We overtire them, we overstrain them, we overfeed them, we do everything that we can, almost, to damage them very often.

"From the point of view of the magnificence of them, the accuracy of the functions that they perform—I don't know if you ever even thought just about walking along the street. How you put one foot in front of the other is absolutely an automatic thing; the number of things that have to work in order to do that. Somebody once worked out, I remember when I was listening to lectures in hospital, that a movement of one's little finger made every muscle in the body readjust itself. This is the way in which it's made. You're certainly fearfully and wonderfully made. How much you want me to go into the mechanics of it, I don't know."

David: "Well, we could spend some hours on it. There are those who say this body, as wonderful as it is, is the result of chance, it's just the result of atoms behaving in mutation by sheer chance. Could you believe that?"

Matt: "No, I've never found that this is a theory which is completely true. I think there's some ways in which adaptations take place to suit their environment and I think this in a way has sometimes given rise to a theory which is just about as full of holes as a fishing net. There are many things which cannot be explained in that way. One of the things, of course, is this: where the animal is very 'wise'. I remember once we had a dog and it would just catch food from the table. If somebody threw him a pickled onion, that dog never caught anything from that person again, he'd always let it fall on the ground first and sniff it. The human is much less wise; we make the same mistakes over and over again."

David: "Now let's come to another feature of the body. Both your body and my body are wearing out; they last us maybe seventy, eighty, even ninety or one hundred years, but there is this sad fact that this body doesn't last forever, even though it's better than a car and a fridge the way we treat it, it doesn't last forever. It's been a mystery to many people why the body can't go on replacing itself and just go on living. Have you any thoughts about the body wearing out?"

Matt: "Yes, I know that this is a mystery. The mechanics to some extent is a mystery to the scientists and the physiologists. You see, the body is made so that almost immediately [after] it's born it begins to die. Cells die, but there are mechanics for the replacement, there's a sort of service station which constantly replaces every part of the body. The skin that we rub off every time we touch anything; every time the policeman takes your fingerprints, he takes your fingerprints by your leaving some of your skin on the paper. Every time that this happens it's replaced. This goes right through the body. But for some reason or another, this mechanism gradually fails. I myself feel this is due to something disturbing the perfect balance that was originally intended here.

I think if the balance could be maintained the body could go on forever. But either through our own weakness, our own abuse, we disturb this balance, or I think obviously by heredity sometimes it's disturbed or in other ways by the environment in which we live. Some people who live in too much sunshine, some people who live in too much cold; these things can disturb the balance. But it's an interesting thing, isn't it, that in the first part of Genesis the bodies of the people there lived for a thousand years? In other words, were they nearer the time of complete balance? In Genesis 11, I think there's about six or seven generations [in which] the longevity of the body falls from about six or seven hundred years down to about 120."

David: "But it's only in one family, incidentally; it's not over the whole human race. This confirms a scientist who said recently that there is no scientific reason why a person should die. They still cannot figure this out."

David: "Now let's get on to the subject for this morning, Matt, the new body we're going to have. Do you find this an exciting thought? Do you think about it much? Do you think you'll be a physiotherapist in heaven?"

Matt: "Well, there is a little bit of sadness you see. I'm going to have to learn a new trade, and so incidentally are you."

David: "That's good. Let's go a little further with this, Matt. All of us have handicaps of one kind or another. You have one with your sight, others have hearing, and there are limitations we all have here. Do you find yourself looking forward to a body free from this?"

Matt: "Well, the passage which you read this morning from Paul is one of the great passages that I suppose most of us have looked at in this. The idea of perfection, the absence of pain, the absence of weariness, but much more than that, the abilities that this body is going to give us. There's going to be no imperfections, there's going to be no handicaps, there are going to be no limitations on movement as far as one can understand. We are told that our body will be like Christ's. His was able to go through material, it was able to go up to heaven without any problem at all; the mobility is going to be terrific. But of course, for those of us, I think, who have experienced in life the loss of something, I would say you never know the value of anything until you've lost it. We take too much for granted.

"But I remember I saw a man this Thursday when I was in London for the Royal National Institute for the Blind. He and I first met at college. One of the first things he said to me was that he was born blind. One of the things he said to me was I think one of the most wonderful things I've ever heard. He said, 'Do you realise that the first person that I shall ever see will be Jesus Christ?' This perhaps gives some colour to the extent of the thought of this wonderful situation that's going to pertain."

David: "Yes, well that's a wonderful thought to leave everybody with if they get nothing else.

"I'd like to change to a quite different matter now, Matt. Not only now are you a physiotherapist, you're in the telephone Samaritans. I'm not going to publicise that because you like to do your work anonymously, but nevertheless, you are contacted by people who feel the only way out of their problems is to kill the body. What leads a person to such a desperate decision?"

Matt: "Well, it's very extraordinary. Last night I was talking to someone and we were talking about this very matter. They said to me, 'Look, if life beyond is going to be so much better than here why is it that people, everybody,' they said, 'tends to cling to the life that we've got so hard. They try and keep their life. Why aren't they prepared to let it go?' I said, 'Well as a matter of fact, I spend a bit of my time trying to persuade people to cling to this life and not to just throw it away'.

"But the curious thing is that the people who are always so anxious to throw their life away are the people that have put all their faith in this life, the enjoyments of the riches of this life, these are the people who come to the point where they say, 'The thing isn't what I thought it was going to be, it isn't what I wanted and so I'm going to get out of it.' It's a curious thing that the people who base the whole of their life on what they get from this life, when they find that it isn't what they wanted or what they thought it was going to be, these are the people who tend to get into such a depressed state that they feel that life is no longer worth having and they're prepared to get rid of it. Of course, we would say they're not escaping from anything."

David: "In fact, a belief in something afterwards could be the best thing that could help them to see this life in perspective."

Matt: "Well, I think this is true; so often one finds that the people with a convinced faith concerning the afterlife seem to find their reason and their purpose for living in this one."

David: "Which is a good note to close on. Thank you very much indeed, Matt."

....

I now want to take that much further and take it through the Bible now. In the previous chapter, we talked about what happens to a person when they die and we said that death is essentially the separation of the body from the spirit. The question comes, what happens to body and spirit? Some people say in one word, "extinction," both body and spirit cease to be. Indeed, they might even go on to say that there is no such thing as the spirit at all. It is like the man who dissected a human body to its last item and said, "I couldn't find a soul anywhere." He was just about as silly as a man who would take an organ to pieces to find the music.

Nevertheless, this is one answer that some people give, extinction; body and spirit finished. There is the answer we call "immortality", and this says that while the body finishes, the spirit goes on, set free from the body. A study of the death of Socrates is quite an amazing thing. He took the hemlock, the poison; he was sentenced to death, but given the choice as a free citizen of committing suicide. As he drank the poison, he gathered his disciples around him, spoke to them peacefully, happily about the joys of the spirit set free from a body and died in complete peace. I have heard someone say that Socrates died in a much better frame of mind than Jesus. Now, if Socrates was right in what he said then this is true and Jesus should not have shrunk from what lay ahead, as he did, in Gethsemane. But what Socrates said is not true. The soul apart from the body is not thereby freer.

The third answer that is given is the answer we call reincarnation, which means that the spirit will come back in someone else's body or in another body on earth. The Buddhists believe this and others have accepted the idea of reincarnation—even some church ministers in this country have toyed with it. But the answer the Christian gives is the answer of resurrection, that one day the body and the spirit will be reunited and that will mean perfect freedom, and that is what we look forward to and every time we state our faith we say, "I believe in the resurrection of the body," body and spirit coming together one day.

We talked about the interval between death and resurrection in the last chapter. Let us talk about the actual resurrection. The idea is ridiculous to many people; it was in our Lord's day. There was a group of people called the Sadducees who just could not accept this idea. As I told you before, that is why they were sad you see, and you will remember their name this way. They could not believe that the body would rise again and be reunited with the spirit and they tried to trip Jesus up with this kind of question: "If a woman had seven husbands in this world each one of whom died one after the other what's going to happen in the next, there's going to be an almighty family quarrel, isn't there?" Jesus had to tell them quite simply, and these are his words: "The children of the resurrection are not like that." He used the word "resurrection" in his reply.

The Greeks did not like this idea at all, and I have stood on the Areopagus, or Mars Hill, where Paul spoke to the Greek philosophers, and they listened to him right up to a certain point. They listened to his ideas about God, about judgment, about human life, about conscience, they listened to all that and accepted it and then he used one word that made them laugh. He used the word "resurrection". They believed in the immortality of the soul and the idea of a body coming back to life was so ridiculous that they began to mock and laugh. So, the Greeks could not take it any more than the Sadducees.

Today there are scientists and philosophers who believe the idea of the resurrection must be discarded if Christianity is going to remain a viable option for twenty-first century minds. On the one hand they say, "It's too materialistic, it makes heaven a place," but then that is what Jesus made it. "It makes the afterlife too much like this one," but then if God makes it like that who are we to quarrel? The main reason why they cannot accept it is it makes it too miraculous and people say, "Well, how could God gather together the cells even of a buried person, never mind a cremated person?" And of course, they are limiting God's almighty power when they ask that question.

There is one fact on which we base our belief that one day we will have a new body, and it is a fact that examined historically, even scientifically, according to the laws of the examination of the past, stands up as an established fact, namely that Jesus rose from the dead.

The evidence for the resurrection is better than for most, if not all, events of history of that period. Anybody who will examine it with an open mind ought to come to the right conclusion. It is because the Christian is convinced that Christ rose from the dead with a body and was able to say, "I am not a ghost, I am not a spirit. A spirit doesn't have flesh and bones; give me some fish to eat," cooking breakfast for them on the seashore. It is because of that we dare to believe in the resurrection of the body. He was buried. His spirit and body were separated for three days and three nights. But what happened on the first Easter Sunday proves that the two can be brought together again by God Almighty. The day before he died, he said, "Because I live you shall live also." This is not an isolated event. It is the first of many.

One day Paul was on trial for his life before a man called Felix, and he told this man, "The one thing that put me in this dock is my hope of the resurrection of the just and the unjust." In fact, he was perfectly right because the Sadducees had put him there. This was the one thing because Paul knew perfectly well, and he wrote it down for us, that this is the kingpin of our faith. If Christ did not rise we might as well close our churches. We certainly could not talk about these things in as happy a way as we do if Jesus were still dead, if he was the greatest man who ever lived and like every other great man died too.

I want to discuss two things in this chapter: the resurrection of the just and the resurrection of the unjust. Once again, you cannot escape the fact that whatever the Bible says about the life [that we have] after death it always divides it into two. It doesn't matter where you look in scripture, there is this profound distinction in everything it says about the future ultimately leading to the biggest distinction of all, heaven and hell. But from the very beginning there is this gulf. From the very beginning there are two and only two groups thought of in the Bible and whenever the resurrection of the body is mentioned two groups are mentioned: the just and the unjust.

Now let us look at these two groups and ask what it says about them. First of all, the resurrection of the just. Who are the just? The answer is those accepted by God as being worthy of heaven, of living with him forever, those who are in God's good books. That is putting it very simply. The Bible uses a rather big word at this point, the word "justified" or "justification". I feel that the Pidgin English version of the Bible translates that beautifully. Did you know that there is a Pidgin English version? It has been translated for many areas of the world where Pidgin English is spoken. In place of the word "justified", which is a thoroughly Latinised word and not even an Englishman understands it anyway, it says, "God, 'e say I'm all right." Now that is tremendous. That is what justified means. The just are those of whom God says, "He's all right. She's all right."

Now, how could you possibly enter such a category? How could you get into such a book? How could you possibly be just before God? Well, there are two ways. The first way is to be perfect, that is one way. If you live a perfect life and do everything that is good from the year dot to the year dot, if you do everything you should and nothing that you should not, if you live a perfect life you are just in God's sight. However, if that were the only way to be just in God's sight that would allow one person into heaven and one only, Jesus—the only man of whom God could ever say, "You are just." But the amazing thing is that the Bible puts millions of others in the same category—not because they are perfect but because they have been pardoned, forgiven, because they have voluntarily asked that their case be taken in this life rather than in the next, because they have asked that God bring the judgment into the present and for the sake of Jesus Christ forgive them their sins. According to my Bible, the moment a man does that his case is taken not in the last day but right now and God takes the case and says, "Justified in my sight. All right." That is what forgiveness is and any man who asks for it is just in God's sight.

Therefore, this category of the just includes not only Jesus, who is perfect, but everyone else who for his sake was pardoned. Therefore, it is a mighty big company and one day there is to be a resurrection of the just. Two questions occur: When? and How? When will this happen? Again, the Bible is crystal clear; there is no need for any doubt on this point, though there are some points even regarding this subject that are doubtful. But there is one crystal-clear point here that concerns when Jesus comes again. You knew that, didn't you? You knew that the next great event in world history is the return of Jesus to Earth. Not the day people stand on Mars, not the Third World War, the next great day in world history will be the day Jesus comes back.

Every Christian is looking for that and that is why this event is linked so closely in scripture with the resurrection of the just. Here is a typical statement: "We look for the Lord Jesus, who may change our vile body that it may be fashioned in you according to his glorious body." In other words, we are waiting for him to come because when he comes this will happen—the just will rise. There are many scriptures one could point to here. Another is 1 Corinthians 15, that we read. But I did not read the part of it which says that "Christ rose first, then at his coming those who are his, those who are Christ's" rose. So, once again the two events are linked. We find that 1 Thessalonians 4:16–17 says the same thing: "For the Lord himself will come down from heaven, with a loud command, with the voice of the archangel and with the trumpet call of God, and the dead in Christ will rise first. After that, we who are still alive and are left will be caught up together with them in the clouds to meet the Lord in the air. And so we will be with the Lord forever." [NIV].

Here are so many passages, but we are left in doubt as to *when* Jesus will come back. On his return he will be the same Jesus who went. His return will be in the same manner that he ascended into the clouds. He will come in the clouds and the angels on the day of ascension said it would happen just the same way in the reverse order. As he went, he will come, and yet his second visit to earth will be completely different from his first. When he came the first time he came as a humble baby so that very few realised he was a king. When he came the first time there was a tiny little pinpoint of light in the sky, a star as a symbol of his coming. When he comes again the whole world will know who has come and the symbol described in scripture is not so much a pinpoint of light.

But Jesus said, "When I come again it will be like lightning from east to west." It will be very different. The same Jesus and yet different, the same manner and yet a different manner, the same and yet different, and I want to convey to you that when referring to our Lord's Second Coming you have got to use the terms, "The same and yet different," because now when I ask the question how will we rise? the answer must be the same, the same and yet different, a body related to this one and yet a body different from it.

Now, let us get down to practical things. What sort of

a body? It will be related to this one and there are many ways in which we can say straight away that based on our experiences we already know what it is for one body to change into another. Matt has mentioned, and I believe it is scientifically true, that the body changes many of its cells every seven years, or over seven years the whole body has had a refit. Whether some parts of us remain or not, I do not know, but the cells are being replaced roughly every seven years in normal healthy life. So here already on earth I have not got the body I was born with. I have been changing it from one end to the other. So, the idea of the body changing into another is not completely unknown to us. Young bodies change into old bodies.

Furthermore, if you have done any biology you must know the mystery of the caterpillar and the butterfly. Three changes of body through the chrysalis in between; each body quite a different appearance from the other, yet one is led to the second and the second to the third and we don't think this is extraordinary. Yet it has been a change of body. So, we already know these things from our ordinary life.

Above all, in your gardens Paul says you have got the answer, take a seed, a potato, plant it in your soil, it will rot, it will go back to the dust and if you dig it up in a few months' time it might just be a little husk left. But the amazing thing is that one day in some months' time you will dig up that soil and you will find another body and another and another very like the original one you planted in the earth and yet not that original one. A body that has come from it, and yet the other one has died and gone back to the dust.

So, in your own back garden you have at least one similar event of something being buried in the ground, going back to the dust, and yet from it a new body coming, so we really should have no excuse for saying this is quite out of my imagination. At a funeral service when we bury the mortal remains of someone we have loved I often think we are just planting something in the garden. We expect a body to come from that—like it, yet not the same body; somewhere related to it beyond our understanding and yet a new one.

In what way will it be different? It is to be changed in some way. In a wonderful passage in 1 Corinthians 15 Paul gives us four ways in which the new body will be different from the one I am using at this moment. Here they are. First of all, this body which I use now is a body of corruption. The new one will be a body of incorruption. Let those words sink in. They are again Latinised words, a bit long, a bit polysyllabic, but nevertheless, let us look at what the meaning is. Matt pinched one sentence from my sermon, and that is that the moment you are born you begin to die. This is a fact. I am speaking as a dying man to dying people. I don't mean we have all been to the doctor and had some bad news. I mean the simple fact is that when I was born, I began to die; my cells began to die straight away. We become more and more aware of this; our teeth, our hair, our bones. Hair goes thinner, teeth begin to decay, bones begin to get more brittle; we know perfectly well that we are in a body that is decaying and it is foolish to deny this to oneself or to anyone else. Shakespeare's man "Sans teeth, sans eyes, sans taste, sans everything" is the man we see in the mirror.

We look forward to a body that will not age, that will not grow weaker, that will not decay; a body that will not have to be in this constant battle to overcome the decay that is setting in. A dentist is just spending his life fighting that battle. Because we do not like to fight the battle either with decay or with the dentist, we keep it out of our minds as much as we can, but he is fighting it. So is the physiotherapist, so is the surgeon. We are fighting it. There will be no such thing in heaven. We shall all have new professions. We shall all have to develop new gifts. We shall all have to find some new service. But if the next world is anything like as interesting as this one, and the Bible indicates that it is more interesting, there will be even more wonderful things to do there than here. It is a new heaven and a new earth, incidentally, and the earth will be a wonderful place as well as heaven; the whole universe new. There will be plenty to do, but not for the medical profession.

The second is this is a body of dishonour, but that will be a body of glory. I remember visiting a dear saint in the hospital who had become almost like a child and everything had to be done for him. He turned to me and he said, "You know, I now understand the phrase 'This body of our humiliation.'" He said, "It does hurt my pride to have to let others do things for me now." This body of dishonour, a body that bears in itself the marks of our sin in some way or another, and every person over forty is responsible for their face. This body of ours that shows the marks of what we have been through is a body of dishonour, but the body of glory will be a body like the body of Jesus. It will be a body like his body on the Mount of Transfiguration, which was so glorious they could hardly bear to look at it. We are to be like him, a body of glory.

Now, the third contrast, Paul says, is that this is a body of weakness that will be a body of power. We are very conscious of our weakness, until we get to our prime and then we think we can do anything and we don't need any help, thank you. Then that is soon over and we begin to need help again. We are weak. Even in our prime we are weak and cannot do the things we want to do. Even youth shall faint and be weary, much more so in older ones and little ones. There are physical limitations at both ends of life, but then a body of power. I get the impression from the resurrection stories that Jesus had the power to do anything he wanted, including, as has been mentioned, the power to travel through space. No man has been in space yet except Jesus. Every other man has had to live "in earth" when he went up there. But Jesus had the power over his body to be free to travel; locked doors meant nothing to him. A body of power; we shall have this mobile body of power in its prime.

The fourth contrast is between a physical, natural body and a spiritual body. That does not mean that this is a vague soul floating in a nightdress that you can't get hold of. It means that this body came to me from the flesh; it came to me from the earth; it goes back to where it came from; it is a body that ties me down to this existence. The body I will have there will be a body from above not below. The evolutionists who feel that the only possible source of a body is the long process of evolution are going to be staggered in that day when a body is given to us from above.

It is the difference between coming from below and coming from above. Every skyscraper that man builds has to be built up from below. We look for a city whose builder and maker is God, the New Jerusalem coming down. It is the difference between the way a Christian and an unbeliever thinks. The unbeliever thinks everything has to come up from earth, the believer says, "No, the things that really are worth having come down from heaven, including our new body." So, the first is a body that came from below and goes back, the second is a body given from above that fits me for the realms above. A spiritual body means a body that is free to move wherever the spirit wants to move. That is what is meant, and as I have borne the image of Adam, I shall bear the image of Christ.

One little note here for those readers who are still alive when the Lord Jesus comes back. If this includes you, you are going to have the great thrill of never dying. I find that exciting. Paul hoped that he would be alive to see it, but he was disappointed. Every generation of Christians hopes for this;

we shall not all die. Some of us will, but some of us will still be alive when this day of resurrection comes. What happens to those who are still alive? Well, they will need new bodies. Their old ones cannot inherit the kingdom. So, I tell you a mystery, we shall not all die but we shall all be changed in a moment; in the twinkling of an eye, the dead will be raised incorruptible and we who are still alive shall be changed.

You may have heard that sung in Handel's *Messiah* so often. Did you believe it? It is going to be the noisiest day in history. The archangels are going to be shouting, the trumpets are going to be blowing, with a loud cry Jesus will descend, and it will be loud enough for the dead to hear. We talk about being so loud you could wake the dead. We can't. But Jesus can and will.

So, we have this tremendous thought of two groups of people. I have the feeling that in a verse that is read at most funeral services these two groups are mentioned. Jesus said, "I am the resurrection and the life. He who believes in me though he dies"—there's the number one group—"yet shall he live, but he who lives and believes in me shall never die." It seems to me that there is the other group, "The quick and the dead", as the prayer book refers to them. Here we have the two groups. Those who die believing in Jesus shall live, those who are still living, believing in him shall never die, but we will all be caught up together. What a wonderful thought. What a meeting! That will be the biggest Christian rally you ever attended.

But I must come now to the other and more solemn side of the picture; the resurrection of the unjust. It is quite clear in scripture that everybody will rise from the dead. The unjust are those not accepted by God, which in simple language means those who are not perfect and are not pardoned. I shall say more about this in the next chapter. But let us look now at two questions: when will the unjust rise and how will they rise? First of all, when? Many have assumed that it is the same time as the just.

After a very careful study of scripture, I can only say quite frankly, though I would respect other views, that my examination leads me to believe it will not be at the same time. There is first of all, all our Lord's teaching about one being taken and the other left, which has to be reckoned with and taken into account. That thought has led many a husband to Christ when he realises his wife will be taken and he may be left. But there are many other things. There is this unusual phrase every time the resurrection of the just is mentioned, the phrase "Resurrection out from among the dead," which is used of the Christian as something that will make him different from the others.

There is, furthermore, the statement in 1 Corinthians 15 that the resurrection takes place in three steps: Christ, the first, then at his coming those who are his, and then stage number three, the end. It is quite clear from a reading of scripture that the unjust rise at the end. Furthermore, there is the fact that when the just rise there is no passage that mentions the unjust rising at the same time. When we come to the final book in the Bible there is the clearest statement of all, which talks unequivocally of the first and the second resurrection and says, "Happy are those who share in the first." So, I take it that while resurrection is a fact for everybody, the unjust will be well behind the just in this. I won't go into any more details now.

The other question is how? If the just receive a body that reflects the glory of their real life in Christ, I can only assume that the unjust will be given a body that reflects the real state of their sinful, selfish character. I find that a most frightening thought. Already in this life the older we are the more our real character shows in our body. If we take it that in the saint the beauty of Christ begins to show, in the sinner the horror of Satan begins to show. If the resurrection of the just brings the beauty of the saint to his or her perfection it would seem to me that the resurrection of the unjust could bring the ugliness of sin to its logical conclusion. I think this is what may be referred to in the Bible where it says, "The unjust rise to shame and everlasting contempt."

My conclusion is this. Why do we rise from the dead? The answer is very simple: to make judgment possible both of reward and of punishment. To that we address ourselves in the next chapter. Let Jesus himself have the last word on the subject. Here are his own words from John's Gospel: "For the hour is coming in which all that are in the grave shall hear the Son of Man's voice and shall come forth. They that have done good to the resurrection of life and they that have done evil to the resurrection of damnation." These are the words of Jesus and we shall take the story up from there in the next chapter.

Chapter 4

Judgment

From time to time, every minister takes funeral services. It is part of our calling to minister at times of need like this, and that brings us into contact with a group of people known as funeral directors. It is a great joy to a minister to meet from time to time a Christian funeral director who understands what the minister is seeking to do, what the real need of the situation is, but above all who is in a position to help people at this time of deep need, and often is the first to be in the home and to be able to bring some word of comfort. I am most grateful to Mr Wakefield for coming along this morning. I am going to ask him one or two questions and he will share with you, perhaps, in his answers, some of the insights he has gained, because of all callings, his is one that faces and has to face the fact of death and come to terms with it and seek to help people to face it.

David: "Now Mr Wakefield, I don't know exactly how long you've been a Christian. Could you tell us how long you have been one and how you became a Christian first?"

Mr Wakefield: "Well, I had to look it up in my Bible and I found it. I became a Christian in 1952. I think at this point I ought to say that I became a Christian because someone who was concerned thought I should become a Christian, and people were praying. Then my son, who's now about twenty-three, was about four, we decided that we'd send him to Sunday school, for no reason, except that we really wanted to get him out of the way, I think! But we decided to send him to Sunday school and the little girl as well, who's younger, and of course the contact was made. The pastor at that time, who was an honorary pastor, called on the parents and I happened to be the father. I was called on too. This dear man, he decided that house was to be won for the Lord, and he succeeded just by reading me the Word of God. I hadn't made it into the church at all. I don't think I knew at that time what it looked like inside, except a tiny little chapel. But he did it by reading me the Word of God and persistence, and calling on me once a fortnight, or something like that, over a period of time, and I believe now—but of course I didn't know it at the time—that the prayers of the people led me to the Lord."

David: "Well, that's wonderful to know. Now, you've been a funeral director for longer than that. They used to say undertaker, but that has now gone out with the word work and other things, and I gather the Americans now call themselves senatorial consultants. Well, it's a wonderful calling in the sense that you're really helping people. It's not a calling that many people would choose to have. How did you become a funeral director?"

Mr Wakefield: "Well, originally my father decided I ought to be apprenticed to a trade. Well, I wouldn't call my profession a trade, but anyway, I'd been a cabinet making apprentice. Of course, it involved making coffins. And so, I think I'm one of the only funeral directors that started from the bottom and worked up."

David: "From one point of view, it could be a lonely life. I said in an earlier sermon in this series that people are running away from death, and presumably, therefore, from anything and anyone associated with it. Do you find this?"

Mr Wakefield: "Well, as I said to the people just now, it goes against me. It's not many people that want to know me."

David: "Well now, you have this opportunity to help people. You're meeting them at the point at which they have a very deep-felt need. Answer this honestly. Do you notice any difference when you go into a Christian home after a bereavement?"

Mr Wakefield: "Well, being a Christian, I'm actually sure that there's one that's with them, people who are Christians, and also one of the things that stands out more is at the time of the funeral when I find that people who have a deep faith in our Lord do hold on to that faith and hold on to him. Although, of course, they grieve for their loss, I find that they are not so outwardly grieved and in stark despair as people who have no faith."

David: "How do people who have no faith comfort themselves in such a situation?"

Mr Wakefield: "Well, I think they look around for everything they can find. All the ways of the world, such as drink, but I think they still feel that they haven't really got any satisfaction for quite a long time afterwards."

David: "According to a recent Gallup poll, ninety-eight per cent of the people in this country would like to be buried by a clergyman. It's far from ninety-eight per cent that would like to meet him earlier than this, judging by congregations. It does seem strange to those of us who are ministers that people, ninety per cent perhaps, would prefer to keep out of our hands during their life, but would like us to bury them. Have you any comments to make on that?"

Mr Wakefield: "With due respect, I'm the first one to come before people who have lost someone, and I find that as a Christian I feel that the first thing to do is to point them to someone who can give them the Word of God. I know as a Christian I should really, being evangelical in mind, tell people about our Lord and I do if I get the opportunity, but I feel that God's ministers are there, available and as soon as I can I contact, if it's a person of the Church of England faith, I contact the minister of the parish and I give him details as to when the people will be in, available, and I dare to tell people that the minister will call on them. Of course, if the people are of the faith of a Baptist, they're naturally in contact with their own minister usually. It's mostly people I deal with who are not in contact with any church organisation at all or any minister at all."

David: "I believe you do follow up in a little way yourself afterwards."

Mr Wakefield: "Yes, I do. I send out a card afterwards, a memorial card with the Word of God on it, because I tell people I came to the Lord through the Word of God and I believe the Word of God. I think that if I pass the Word of God on to someone else, they might come the same way as I did."

David: "Now, as a funeral director, you've had to face death very directly, both before you became a Christian and after. What was your first reaction to this? Was it to shrink or to become hard?"

Mr Wakefield: "Well, I don't think I've ever become hardened. I certainly treat death with respect.

"I know the Word of God says it's the last enemy, and it is an enemy, I believe, and I treat it with respect. In the Old

Testament, they used to sacrifice a calf and sprinkle the burnt ashes on the water and they were cleansed after they'd come in contact with death, but I feel now that being close to our Lord Jesus Christ, he cleanses me and keeps me cleansed from any adverse effect of it."

David: "Do you find it easy to believe in a life after death?"

Mr Wakefield: "When I became a Christian, I was taught to believe this word. I find I'm always reminded about it because nearly every other service I go to is 1 Corinthians 15. If anybody wants to know what I'm talking about, let them read it to themselves, and the Lord says that there is an after death—so says Paul."

David: "Finally, what would you say to those who are unwilling to face death, to think about the future? Have you any word that you'd like to pass on?"

Mr Wakefield: "Well, it is always on my mind that people, whether they're young or old, never know when they're likely to be taken from this earth. I feel that people are not concerned enough about eternal life and they really should be; those who are not concerned should be concerned; they should be close to our Lord Jesus Christ and know him as their personal Saviour and friend. I feel that is not just as an insurance policy, but if they've got faith in Christ and know him, they've also got someone to rest their faith on and trust in and place it with their feet on a rock; for the ills and troubles of this present life, apart from eternal life hereafter."

David: "Well, thank you very much, Mr Wakefield. You have in your job obviously to be serious most of the time and that tends to get funeral directors a name for being gloomy.

It's been a great joy to meet you and see something of the Christian joy in you."

Mr Wakefield: "I'd like to read out just before I finish what's on my card that I send out."

David: "Yes, do. They'd be most interested."

Mr Wakefield: "I can't read it till I put my glasses on."

David: "This is a card you send out how long after?"

Mr Wakefield: "Well, as soon after as I can."

David: "Yes, you read it to us."

Mr Wakefield: "It's from Romans 8:38–39: 'For I am persuaded that neither death nor life, nor angels nor principalities nor powers, nor things present nor things to come, nor height nor depth, nor any other creature shall be able to separate us from the love of God, which is in Christ Jesus our Lord.' That's what's on the card."

David: "Well, thank you very much for coming. It's been lovely to have you."

....

In the letter to the Hebrews 9:27 we read: "it is appointed unto men once to die, but after this the judgment". There are two appointments which every man and woman in the world has, neither of which may be put in a diary because the date is not known. The first appointment is the day we die,

JUDGMENT

and while it would be wonderful to be able to put that in the diary and prepare for it, many of us cannot. Perhaps it is a merciful providence that enables us to live in the uncertainty of that. The other appointment we have is equally uncertain as to the date, but it will most certainly occur, and after that comes the judgment.

Everybody knows the first appointment is coming, but if you leave that by itself and consider only that, then your reaction will be to live it up: "Eat, drink and be merry, for tomorrow we die." If that is the only appointment we have got in the future then let's make the most of the here and now. Let's live it up while we can. This is what many people are doing. As I have mentioned before, a Gallup poll among sixth-formers in Surrey revealed that over half of them did not think that they would live to see middle or old age; that the world would have been blown to bits before then. Therefore, they aimed to live it up right then. If you want to know the reason behind some of the crazy behaviour of youth, this is it.

But once you consider the second appointment that follows the first, far from living it up, you will find this sobering. This chapter's subject is judgment. Now this is not a very nice subject; it is not a very comforting one; it is not a very helpful one from one point of view. The great temptation when we are talking about life after death is to rush on to the nice bit. It would be much nicer for me to give you six chapters on heaven, which I could have done and would gladly have done, but it would not have been the whole truth. Heaven will seem all the sweeter when we talk about it in the final chapter, for having faced the realities that come first.

By way of introduction, let me say two things. First of all, the necessity of judgment is written into life. It is absolutely necessary that there should be some sorting out, some compensation, some reckoning in the future. Why should it be necessary? For two reasons. First of all, because of the injustice of life; the fact is that in this world many wicked people do prosper and many good people do suffer. Life itself demands some kind of sorting out, some kind of levelling up, some kind of putting things straight and putting things right. This life taken by itself is not just. It is not fair. It is not balanced. Once we study the facts of children suffering in this world, that is enough to tell us that the injustice of life demands judgment. It is not right that Napoleon and Father Damien, King Herod and John the Baptist, Jezebel and Mary, and Hitler and Albert Schweitzer should ultimately come to the same end, and our instinct demands that somewhere beyond death all the wrongs should be righted.

There is another reason why judgment is necessary and it is the justice of God; not just the injustice of life, but the justice of God. If God is good, then he must put things right. If we dare to say that God is just, then because life is unjust there must be beyond death an expression of God's justice. If he is good and if there were no judgment in the future, I could not believe in a good God. Regarding people who say to me, "How do you expect me to believe in a good God when the world is like this?" if there is no judgment in the future, you could not. If we limited our sights to this life, we could not believe in a fair God, but the Bible repeatedly makes the point that someday in the future whatsoever a man has sown that shall he also reap, because God is not mocked.

Now, the second thing by way of introduction is this: not only is judgment necessary, but a day of judgment is also necessary. Why? Why could God not judge each of us the day we die? Why does he have to save it all up for a big day in which judgment will take place? Of course, Christians have never believed that we are judged as soon as we die. There is a waiting period until the resurrection, then the Day of Judgment. Why a day? The answer is very simple, and it is that justice must be public.

Now, if ever you have had the experience, as I hope you have had—you have the right to have it and you should take advantage of the right—if you have ever had the experience of sitting in a court of law, you will know that you were perfectly free to go in and sit in the public gallery. Why? Because there is a deep-rooted instinct in British justice that justice must be public, that it must be seen to be right, that it must be witnessed by all, that it must not be secret, that it must not be hidden. However painful and difficult it is for those immediately concerned, I would not like to see the public galleries abolished from our law courts, because in a country where there are secret trials that are not open to the public, it is because there is a totalitarian regime that is afraid to let people see what is happening for fear they would see that it is not just.

Justice must be public and seen to be so, and therefore the Bible makes quite clear that God's judgment will be public for all to see. Why? For three reasons—first, God must be vindicated. God must be seen by everybody to be just. At the moment, a lot of people do not see this. They say, "God is unjust. God is unfair. Why does he do this? Why does he allow that?" There must be a day in which everybody looks at God and says, "He is fair. He is just." He must be vindicated. Christ must be vindicated publically. The last time the world saw Christ on a day of judgment, they saw him condemned as a criminal. There must be a day in which Christ is seen publically to be right and just and fair.

Christians must be vindicated. The world has been very unfair to Christians. There has not been a period of ten years over the last two thousand years in which Christians have not been martyred because they belong to Jesus. Christians must be vindicated. There must come a day when they are seen to be God's people publically, and therefore this fact of a day of judgment is written into the Bible. You can't read the Bible without coming across it. It is there in the Old Testament prophets; it is there in the New Testament epistles. Above all, it is right there in almost every story that our Lord told.

You study the parables of Jesus, those amazing stories which are so deep in truth that you could go on studying them for a lifetime and never get to the bottom of them, and again and again the story builds up to a day. The wheat and the tares grow together until a day comes when they are separated. The sheep and the goats graze together until a day comes when they are separated. The wise and foolish virgins are together until a day comes, a moment comes, when they are separated. The good and the bad fish caught up in the fishing net are caught up together until the day when they are sorted out and distinguished. So many stories of Jesus finish up with the day when the sickle is put into the harvest, when some crisis comes which divides what has formerly been together.

Now let us look at this Day of Judgment as a trial, as a courtroom. That is how we are told to look at it in scripture. First of all, let us look at the judge. Who is there sitting on the bench today? Having been in courts from time to time, I have noticed that so often this is a crucial factor. Who are the JPs today? It is so and so—he is a bit tough, or she is a bit soft and so the word goes around. Who is it today? It is a vital question. Who is going to try me? Who is going to take this case? The obvious answer would be God the Father, but it would be the wrong answer, because for this great day the Father has delegated the responsibility for judgment to someone else. That is the Bible teaching, and he has delegated it to a human being, to a man. A man is going to judge the human race—someone who knows what it is to be human; someone who has known all the pressures and all the problems of living a human existence, and his name is Jesus.

JUDGMENT

Listen to Paul preaching in Athens, the centre of the intellectual world of those days: "God has appointed a day in which he will judge the world by a man—Christ Jesus." Jesus is still a man. We must not forget that. He did not become a man for thirty-three years, but for eternity, and when he appears on the bench on this day he will appear as a man, for he is a man. It will be a man who judges the human race. I find it very intriguing and indeed, awe-inspiring to realise that on that day, Jesus sitting on the bench will confront Pontius Pilate in the dock. Those who have judged Jesus through the ages and said what they thought of him will find that the crucial question is what he says and thinks of them—a reversal of the situation we read in the Gospels.

Now then, who are the prisoners? The answer is all the human beings who have ever lived, great and small, kings and slaves, dead and alive, those who have been drowned in the sea will be there. We are told that specifically in the Bible. Those who have been buried in the earth will be there. Everybody will be there. Here is a very important point. Each person will be dealt with personally. I suppose it would be some comfort to some if we were going to be dealt with in blocks, in nations, but it is crystal clear from scripture. Don't ask me how God can do this. I cannot explain how God can have a trial dealing with each one personally in a day of judgment and having sat for hours in court waiting for someone's case to be brought up, I just don't know how he can do it. I don't know how he knows the number of hairs on my head, but I just know he is God.

He will manage it, but he will most certainly deal with each one personally. Anything less than that would be unjust. At school, when the headmaster or the form master kept us all in and punished us because of what one boy had done, instinctively we felt that it was unjust, unfair. It would be equally unfair if God did the same thing, so we are told in the

Bible, quite simply, that every one of us shall give account of himself. You will not have to give account of anyone else, only yourself. He will deal with each one personally and directly. We will give account for no one's life but our own. That should make us more concerned about our own standards than about anyone else's.

The third thing: what evidence will be brought? Well, let us say first of all, that the evidence of appearance will be worthless on that day. Unfortunately, we all judge each other by our appearance. We are bound to. That is the part we see. We judge each other by what we see, but we are told that the Lord does not look at the outward appearance, but at the heart. It is the inside of us, not the outside of us that he will be concerned with.

We are told that it will not be the evidence of our profession—what we say. "Not everyone that says to me, 'Lord, Lord,'" said Jesus. "Not everyone." It is not what we say. You may have sung hymns. You may have said prayers. Profession, what we say, is not the evidence he will use. We are told that he will not use the testimony of other people. There will be no witnesses for the defence, because God knows everything that there is to know. We will not be able to say, "Well, would you just hear from my next-door neighbour? I've helped her quite a bit and she'll put in a good word for me." God knows the evidence perfectly. There will be no testimonies. There will be no quibbles over technicalities of the law, because we are dealing with a perfect law. There will be no loopholes, no quibbles that can ease the situation.

What evidence will be used? We are told this, that books will be opened. What will be in those books? What evidence will be in them? The answer is very simple. All that we have done in the body are works. Now let me explain this word "works". It does not mean just our good deeds. It means everything we have done and said and felt that was an expression of our real character; not just when we were on duty or on show, but everything we have said and felt and done that expressed what we really were.

That is why one of the most frightening things I think Jesus ever said was that we would be judged for our idle words. He meant by that the occasional slips of the tongue that came out and revealed what we were really like. This is the evidence that will be taken—everything that has expressed our real character. It has been recorded in books. As our Lord said, that means many secret things will be revealed. Things that were done and said in the bedchamber will be shouted from the housetops. Things that other people didn't know about us will come out on that day as evidence.

Now the fourth question: by what standard will this evidence be tested? What is the pass mark? As an RAF chaplain I used to have great fun with the recruits, the boy entrants who came in and had to appear before a padre before they went on to their training. I used to ask how many Methodists there were and how many Baptists there were, and so on. They used to put their hands up and then I would say, "And how many Christians are there?" They would look so hesitant and some of them would look to see if anybody else would put a hand up.

Occasionally one did, and by a look at the face I knew that they knew what I meant, but usually the others said, "Well, what do you mean by a Christian?" I would say, "Well, what do you think a Christian is?" They would say, "Oh well, somebody who keeps the Ten Commandments." It is amazing how often that came up, so I used to say, "Fine, a Christian is someone who keeps the Ten Commandments; how many Christians here?" and again there was hesitation. "Oh well, no one can keep them all, Padre." "All right then. What's the pass mark? How many do you have to keep?" They nearly always settled after a considerable discussion for six out of ten, and so I would say, "Fine, a Christian is someone who keeps six out of ten commandments. How many Christians are there here?"

What is the pass mark? What is the standard? The answer is very simple, but many people seem to have difficulties at this point. It is just not necessary to think in this way. The answer is the revealed will of God is the standard. To go one step further, we shall each be judged by how much of the revealed will of God we knew—no more, no less. It would obviously be utterly unjust for God to judge someone on what they never knew. We have an assurance in scripture written there in black and white in Romans 2 that such a thing will never happen. What we are told is that everybody will be judged according to the light they have received. Nothing could be fairer.

Now let us look briefly at three main groups of people in this regard to see it clearly. First of all, those who have heard about Jesus Christ and known about Christian standards will be judged by Christian standards and by Jesus Christ. So many people say to me, "What about those who've never heard?" My answer is, "Well, you have heard, and it's you who must render your account." You can leave them to God, but if you have heard you will be judged by that. You will not be judged in the same way as they will be judged, but if you have heard about Jesus, if you have heard that he died to save you, and that he desired you to be his disciple and you have refused to be that, you will be judged by that, so that there is what might be called "Christendom".

I would include Britain in this and the majority of people in this country who still come back to the clergymen to bury them. Most people in this country seem to have at least some basic knowledge of Christian things still. They have had ten years of it at school. I know that God will allow for the kind of teaching they got at school, but they have had it. They have heard of Jesus and there is a church at almost every street corner. We shall be judged by that. "How shall we escape if we neglect so great a salvation?"

Then there are the Jews who have not had what we have had, but we are told that those who have had the Ten Commandments will be judged by the Ten Commandments. Every Jew has had that. Then there is the heathen world, and people say, "Well, what about them?" The answer is they have not had the gospel of Jesus Christ, many of them. They have not even had the Ten Commandments, but they have had two things from God which have revealed himself to them. They have had creation. The things that God has made are enough to tell them there is a power greater than themselves to whom they should bow, and they have all had a conscience. This has been God's revelation within them of at least some difference between right and wrong, and they will be judged by the light they have received according to creation outside them and conscience inside. There is not a man on earth who does not have a conscience of some kind and he will be judged by it, so that, in fact, God's test of our life will be how far we have been rightly related to him and to each other according to the light that we had.

Now that is a fair, just, straightforward case, but quite frankly, it worries me stiff because I have never yet met a man who could look me in the face, however ignorant of Christian things he was and say honestly and sincerely, "I have always lived up to the light I had. I have followed my conscience. I have responded to truth as I saw it." There is not a man or woman who can do that, and therefore Paul is right in concluding that God will judge by the light that we have received and by that light we all stand guilty before God. It is as simple and straightforward as that.

If people ask, "Why do we need to send the gospel overseas?" this is why. If they were in a state of innocence before God, then to take the gospel to them would damn them. It would send many to hell who were not going there because it would make them guilty of rejecting the light, but the Bible states they have light and they have already rejected it and therefore need desperately the forgiveness that comes through Jesus Christ. That is the heart of missionary work. It is the heart of evangelism. That is why we preach Jesus, because while in theory if any man lives up to the light he has God will accept him in that day, in practice, none of us has done so. Nor can we blame our heredity and environment. We must all say, even to some degree, that we are responsible for the people we have become, that not one of us is the man or woman we might have been had we perfectly responded to what we knew to be right.

This leaves us in a state of guilt. Like Belshazzar, we are weighed in the balances and found wanting, and yet we are told in the scripture that a great number of people are to be acquitted. Indeed, it goes further and says a great number of people will never even reach the dock and will, in fact, be sitting on the bench helping the Judge. Here we come to the most extraordinary statement in the Bible, I think—that there will be a great many people who will be sitting on the bench with Jesus to judge the world. These are people who are not to be condemned, but acquitted, or in the language of the Roman law courts, justified.

Why should this be? The answer is that there is another book to be opened. The books that I have mentioned already are the books recording our real character as expressed in thought, word and deed, but there is another book to be opened on that day and it is called the Lamb's Book of Life. It is a book that belongs to Jesus and in which only he can write. It is a book containing the names of many people—including, I hope, your name. If not, it will be no one's fault but yours that your name is not in that book.

JUDGMENT

It is a book of those who have asked that their case be taken earlier. It is a book of those who have deliberately asked God not to wait till the Day of Judgment before dealing with sin, but to take it right now, to take the case early. Not with the hope of being acquitted because the good deeds outweigh the bad deeds and that somehow we might just get past that pass mark, but with the knowledge that Jesus Christ died that we might be acquitted, justified, forgiven freely. That is what the cross is all about. That is the heart of it.

God does not want to punish us, so God does not take any delight in paying people back. God does not have any joy in the death of one wicked person. God is a God of love and mercy as well as of justice, and he longs to take people's case early and to acquit them. He longs to do that, but if he did it without the cross he would not be a just God. If he simply overlooked and winked at our sins and said, "Well, there, there, boys will be boys. We'll forgive and forget," I could never say he was good. I might say he was nice, but I could never say he was good. He had to find some way in which justice and mercy could be satisfied together, and he found it in the cross. That is why he is able to take your case now. You can plead that all the sins you have ever done and all those you are going to do can be taken into account and dealt with now. Once you have obtained an acquittal from a court, with all that you have done taken into account and freely confessed, once you have that acquittal you can never again be charged with the same offence.

This is the gospel. This is the good news for those who know that when the day comes for them to stand naked before God, and all that they have expressed in life of their real self is brought out into the public, they don't stand a ghost of a chance of getting acquitted in that day, but can nevertheless humbly say, "God, for the sake of Jesus Christ will you take my case now? Will you take into account all that I've ever done and because Jesus died in my place to deal with those things, will you accept that your justice is satisfied by his death and may I plead for your mercy?" Every man or woman or young person who does that will have their name written in another book—the Lamb's Book of Life, and that book will be opened on the great day.

Does this mean that Christians will never come into judgment? Well, into the judgment of punishment, yes, it does mean that. "There is now therefore no condemnation to them that are in Christ Jesus." Nothing could be clearer, but there is a kind of judgment, if you can call it that, for Christians, for purposes of reward, not punishment. Christ will test our service for him, not to stop us going to heaven— we shall get there—but for purposes of rewarding us in heaven. Our position in heaven, our responsibilities there will depend on our faithfulness since we became Christians here, and that is mentioned in more than one passage in the New Testament. So, a Christian is not someone who goes dancing down the street shouting, "You're all going to hell. I'm not. You're all going to be judged. I'm not. I can do anything I like now." A Christian is one who is so grateful for the acquittal that he has received, and so mindful that his service is still to be tested and rewarded accordingly, that in the fear of God he passes his time of sojourning here in faithful service.

This, then, is the fact of judgment, the second appointment, which every man has, and here is the way to take that appointment now, to get it dealt with now so that never again will it be brought up against you. "And I saw the dead, small and great, stand before God." This is the writer of the last book of the Bible. "And the books were opened, and another book was opened, which is the Book of Life, and the dead were judged." In the next chapter we shall go on with this study and look at this thing called hell. What does it really mean? Then, in the chapter after that, to quote Charles Wesley in a lovely hymn, "the waves divide, and land us all in heaven".

Chapter 5

Hell

The subject of this chapter is hell. Readers' reactions to this word may vary tremendously. To the British workman the word "hell" may simply be a swear word that he uses when he hits the wrong nail with a hammer. To people living in Texas the word "hell" brings to their mind a small oil town which is called "Hell" and which tourists love to visit so they may send a postcard with that postmark on it. "Here we are in Hell having a lovely time," sort of thing. In British Colombia there is a deep, dark valley called "Hell" and there are people living in it. Some of them have chosen to do so for the novelty.

To the Anglo-Saxons, among whom this word originated, "hell" meant quite simply a hidden place. It was used, for example, of the hollow under a tailor's bench where he threw all the scraps of material he didn't need—it was simply a hidden place. It was used by lovers as a secret trysting place where they could be unseen by others. The word "hell" as it originated in the English language simply meant somewhere you cannot see, a hidden place, or a dark place.

You can begin to see how it became attached to certain other ideas, but I suppose to the Western world generally the word "hell" signifies something much more serious than that, because we have been heavily influenced by Dante's poetry, and Milton's, and by Dürer's paintings. We have a picture of hell, part of which may well be true and part may not be true. There have been certain embellishments by the human imagination.

In this chapter, I am not concerned with some of the embellishments. I am not concerned with either the temperature of hell or the furniture of heaven. I am not concerned with the kind of jokes about red-hot ice cream and the rest of it, which I am quite sure you have heard as well as I did both at school and at work. I am concerned with the reality. Now, the idea that in the afterlife there is a good place for good people and a bad place for bad people is something that had gripped the human mind long before the New Testament was written.

Deep down in human nature there is an instinctive belief that after we die there is some kind of distinguishing between the good and the bad, and that there are two places awaiting in the future—one of which is a place of unending bliss and the other a place of unending torment. Plato, for example, describes these two places, giving them two names. "Elysium" is the name he gives to the happy place, and you may have heard about the Elysian Fields, but to the other place he gave the word "Tartarus". It is rather interesting that that word is used in the New Testament, though it was originally coined by a pagan philosopher. The New Testament seems to give approval to an idea which began outside the Bible.

I am going to define hell for the moment as a place of conscious torment where the wicked are punished forever. I am going to ask, "Is it possible, is it right for Christians to hold such a dreadful idea today in the twenty-first century?" I am going to approach it from three angles. First of all, from an intellectual angle dealing with some of the arguments that have been used on both sides; then I am going to approach it from a biblical or scriptural angle to ask, "What does the Bible actually say?" And then, thirdly, I am going to approach it from a practical angle with the question "What difference does it make to your daily life whether you believe in this or not?"

Take first, then, the intellectual approach. Now, there can be little doubt that the majority of people in today's society have rejected belief in hell. I have talked to many people about this subject and it seems quite clear that the majority of people in Britain no longer believe in the idea as I have defined it. There have been so many objections raised to the idea of hell and certain alternative ideas have been proposed in its place.

I picked up an old book in a second-hand bookstore some time ago called *Is There a Hell?* In fact, it was published in 1913 and it was produced by about a dozen Protestant and Roman Catholic ministers and out of that dozen there were only two in 1913 who believed in hell as I have defined it — the rest raised the objections. If that was the case in 1913 it has gone even further today. I remember a gathering of ministers of the church discussing this. I discovered very quickly that out of all the ministers present representing all denominations only the Roman Catholic priest and myself still believed that there was any place that could be called "Hell".

Now, if the ministers of the church have stopped believing in this, I think it would be a fair guess that most of the people they teach have. If most of the people they teach have I think one could say almost certainly that the vast majority of people outside the church also have. What are the reasons for this modern run from the idea? Well, here they are and I give you six objections that have been raised which are very sincerely held and very plausible and very logical.

First of all, and this is not the logical one, there are those who object to the idea of hell on sentimental grounds — they don't like the idea, full stop. Now, I am afraid I am not going to treat this one very seriously because sentiment plays havoc with our belief. If we allow our feelings to control what we believe then, frankly, we shall finish up in a jungle or a desert and we shall change our beliefs constantly. If I say I will not believe a thing because I don't like the idea, then I will have to close my mind to a great many of the facts of life. Many of the facts of life are unpleasant and sentimentalists do not like to face them. That is then no objection, but it is perhaps behind a lot of people's refusal to study carefully the question of hell.

Now, coming to a more serious one, the idea of hell has been objected to on psychological grounds, on the ground that it produces fear and that fear is an unhealthy motive and therefore it is not to be used. Therefore, the idea of hell, which of itself is bound to produce fear, must be wrong—that is the psychological objection. It could be answered that, in fact, fear can be a very healthy thing. If it becomes a phobia then that paralyses action, which is unhealthy, but fear of the traffic and fear of fire and fear of many things is quite healthy if it produces the right action. If it becomes a phobia in which you cannot think of anything else and in which you are panicking and paralysed with fear then it is unhealthy, but this is the psychological objection. This objection more than any other has stopped preachers dealing with this subject for fear they will just send their congregation into neurotic or psychotic states as the result of preaching rather than bring them to the Saviour.

Thirdly, there is a social objection to the idea of hell and this objection runs like this: we have departed in society from the idea of punishment for its own sake, which we call retribution. We now only punish for either reasons of deterrence or reformatory reasons, either to stop others doing this or to reform them, and it is quite obvious that hell could do neither. Therefore, on sociological grounds, if we do not believe in punishment for its own sake in our society how could God possibly be worse than we are?

A fourth objection is a moral objection: hell is not fair, runs this objection. It is surely unjust if for a few sins in a short life a man is punished eternally, so that the punishment is therefore out of all proportion to the crime and is not just or fair—that is the moral objection.

Fifthly, there is a philosophical objection. This objection is that if there is a hell then God has failed. Evil is eternal and the Almighty God has failed to deal with and remove evil and evil will be as everlasting as he is—that is the philosophical objection.

Finally, there is a theological objection, which is this: if God is a God of love how could he send anyone to hell—surely it is a denial of love to do such a thing to a living human being. That is an argument that is perhaps the one that has been used most within the church.

Without dealing at this stage with these attacks, these objections that have been made, let me just add an interesting observation. Nearly every one of the cults and sects with which we have to try and cope—many of which originated in America in the nineteenth century and have not spread over here—has attacked the idea of hell and dismissed it. The Jehovah's Witnesses do not believe in hell, the Christian Scientists do not, the Spiritualists do not. I find it very interesting that these cults do not. One of the reasons for their attraction has been that they have got rid of what Christians have believed for two thousand years.

I suppose among the churches today, the Catholics and Evangelicals are two groups still holding to the traditional definition of hell, but probably most others in between have now disregarded it. Now, if hell is dismissed what do you put in its place? If the world is to have justice in it there must be some kind of alternative, otherwise the whole universe becomes terribly unjust.

There are three alternatives that I have come across; most others are adaptations of these. Number one is the one you will find the man in the street holds, that hell is self-imposed suffering in this life. In simple language, you make your own hell here, you live in your own hell, because you have made it. It has nothing to do with God at all. God does not send anyone to hell, you put yourself there, and you put yourself there in this life. There isn't a hell after death to face, there isn't a God to face who will send you there, it is all here and of your own making. Therefore, it can be of your own unmaking too. Many people have told me quite frankly, "I believe in a hell, but it's the hell you make for yourself here. It's a hell you have to live in as a result of your own actions." The one big snag with this view is that there are many people who ought to be in that kind of a hell who are not. There are many people who are in it who have done nothing to deserve it. But this is the first alternative.

The second alternative, which does accept life after death, whereas the first one does not, is to say that ultimately in some distant future God will save everybody. This is perhaps the view most commonly taught in churches today where the traditional view has been rejected. This belief that God will someday bring everybody to himself is called "universalism". The idea is that God will find a way, if not in this life then in the next, to bring every single person to himself. My biggest difficulty here is frankly the free will of man. If man is free to accept or reject, then God has limited his own freedom to that degree that if he forces everybody to come to heaven then he is not treating them as human beings—that is my difficulty, but this is the second alternative.

The third alternative, which is becoming much more seriously thought about, though it was mentioned a long time ago, is what is called "conditional immortality" or "annihilation", meaning that the wicked will be extinguished altogether, and only the righteous will live forever. The wicked will go out of existence completely. This is the belief that at some point after the Judgment the good will live on, but the wicked will absolutely forever cease to be.

Quite frankly, this reduces very considerably the aspect of punishment. The most that a wicked person could fear would be a lecture from the Judge before they disappear. If this is so, then from my own personal experience I have discovered that extinction is no punishment at all and that most people would prefer extinction. Indeed, I have even had someone go as far as to say to my face, "I would prefer extinction to being in heaven. The idea of being with God and his people forever horrifies me." Extinction, therefore, would be no punishment if that were all there was.

Now, that has approached it from a kind of intellectual point of view, it has looked at the objections, the alternatives suggested. How do we begin to answer this? The answer, surely, is that the Christian, but not anybody else, wants to know what the Bible actually says. If this is the Word of God then God is in a better position to know and we must first of all ask, "What has he said?" But we must be very careful to study the Bible properly. The fact that we have had hellfire preachers in the past who embellished and exaggerated should warn us against preaching or believing what the Bible does not say, however lurid, or in a kind of sadistic way, attractive such embellishments are. On the other hand, we must be careful to see all that the Bible does say.

Now let us look at the scriptural approach for a moment. The first surprise that many will find is this: there is hardly anything about hell in the Old Testament. That is a surprise because many people say that the Old Testament is the severe part of the Bible. That is the bit where God is painted as a God who really punishes and who really lets you have it, the idea that the Old Testament is about a God who punishes, the New Testament is about a God who forgives.

Quite frankly, my doctrine of hell could not be built on the Old Testament because there is hardly anything there. There is a lot about Sheol or Hades, the world of departed spirits, the in-between, but hardly anything about hell in the whole of the Old Testament, so when we ask what the Bible says we have got to start more than halfway through.

When we come to the New Testament, we find another most surprising thing. We find that there is hardly anything about hell in the epistles. Those who think that Paul was guilty of taking the nice religion of Jesus and adding a lot of Jewish strictness to it will be utterly confounded on this subject. Those who think that Paul loved to dangle people over the pit in his preaching will discover that this is not so. Well then, where did we get our idea of hell? The answer is utterly simple: from the lips of Jesus.

If you cut out the things that Jesus said, you would be hard put to it to build up a belief in hell. Why should such a thing be? The answer, I think, is very simple: God wanted us to have it from his Son direct. It is as if this was too terrible, too deep a doctrine to trust to anyone else. It was as if he wanted to say, "I want the person whom you will be convinced is kinder, more loving, more merciful than anyone else who has ever lived, I want him to tell you about hell, because I doubt if you will believe it from anyone else."

Just imagine a Bible in which Jesus says nothing about hell and it all came from Jeremiah and Paul. I can guess what would happen. I can guess what would be said. People would say, "There you are, my religion is the religion of Jesus, these men have twisted it because of their narrow minds and their strict natures," but in fact it was the loving, kind, merciful Saviour who spoke about this subject. Out of all the references I have looked up to prepare this chapter the vast majority come from the first three Gospels (Matthew, Mark, and Luke).

HELL

I am going to go through one or two of his sayings. The decisive issue for Christians is not philosophical, moral or psychological, or any argument of man, but rather the question of whether Jesus is the Truth when he says, "If a thing were not so I would have told you." Do we believe that or not? Is he the Lord of my mind? Somebody once said this to me when I questioned something in the Gospels, and I have never forgotten it: "If Jesus is your Lord, then you accept what he says is true whether your mind says it is or not, but if you only accept his sayings when your mind agrees with them you are lord not Jesus."

If I only accept the things in this Bible that my mind agrees with then I am making myself lord of the Bible and this is the real issue that I found when I studied this, and I confess quite frankly that my own mind, my own temperament, my own nature could not accept hell. The reason why I teach it to you as true is that Jesus must be Lord of my mind. I must believe that his mind is much more logical than mine, and much more able to see the truth than mine is. Call it mental suicide if you like, call it a submission if you like, but I believe the only way to truth is to submit to the one who said, "I am the Truth."

Now, what did he say? I am going to build what I have to say around just two or three texts of his. There are others that one could take, but there isn't space here. Here is the first: "Do not fear those who can kill the body, but cannot kill the soul. Rather fear him who can destroy both body and soul in hell." That is utterly simple English—it comes from our Saviour, it comes from the Lord Jesus. I want to work backwards through the text.

Take the last word, the word "hell", the word that he used in fact was not that word, which is an Anglo-Saxon word, as you may know, it was the word *Gehenna*. If you have been to the Holy Land you have probably seen this place. I have walked through it. Gehenna, or the Valley of Hinnom, is a deep valley that runs round two sides of the city of Jerusalem. It is a deep dark valley and at the bottom of it there is a point where the sun never reaches, always in shade.

Now, this shady valley used to be a place for summer residences of the kings of Israel. Then it became a place of culture. Then it became a place of pagan worship and shrines were erected; black magic and occult activities took place, and it finally became so defiled a place that people were killing and burning their own children to pagan gods within sight of the city of God.

A godly young boy king called Josiah, who came to the throne at the age of twelve, saw how wrong that was and he defiled the valley and he commanded that no one should live in it. He stopped the abominations taking place and he called it Topheth, the Valley of Spitting. From that day onwards, it became the rubbish dump, the garbage heap of Jerusalem. Anything that was not wanted was tossed over the wall, fell into the valley, and there two things happened to the rubbish: worms and maggots ate what was edible and bonfires were kept burning to destroy the rest.

By the time of our Lord, when a criminal was executed his body was thrown into that valley and our Lord's own body would have been thrown there if Joseph of Arimathea had not intervened. Furthermore, it was down in the depths of that valley that a man called Judas hanged himself and went to his own place. Now, when our Lord spoke of hell he always used this name Gehenna, a place for rubbish, a place of burning, a place of worms, a place associated with sin and with crime—it is a vivid picture.

The next phrase, working back, is "body and soul," and it is quite clear that he is referring to something after the resurrection when body and soul have been reunited. He said that although somebody may kill your body, you are not to be afraid because if they do, that is not the worst thing that can happen to you. You would think the way some people talk that it is indeed the worst thing that could happen. But somebody killing your body is not the worst thing that can happen; there is something even worse that can happen to body and soul together later. So, our Lord is clearly talking about the ultimate future.

The word "destroy" needs looking at. At first sight, it looks as if it means "to make extinct, to annihilate, to rub out altogether", but I want to tell you that careful study has shown all scholars—they are all agreed on this—that the word does not necessarily mean that. It is used of something that is ruined, that is wasted, that has become useless, or lost; it is used of the lost sheep in the parable of the lost sheep; it is used of the withered wine skin when new wine was put into it. It was also used by Judas when the woman poured the ointment on Jesus, which Judas viewed as a waste.

When you study the word "destroy", the word "perish", it means in scripture precisely this: to be rendered useless, to be wasted, and to be ruined. That is exactly how we use the word perished today. If you talk about a hot water bottle that has perished what do you mean? That it has gone out of existence? That it has ceased to be? No. You mean that it has become wasted, ruined, and is now useless for the purpose for which it was made. What do you do with it when you reach that stage? The answer is quite clear: it goes in the dust bin. There is nothing else you can do with something that has perished—nothing at all.

If something is broken, that is all right, you can mend it, but if something has perished it has become useless and you can only throw it away. The Valley of Gehenna outside Jerusalem was simply full of perished stuff. I believe that Jesus Christ has the power to mend broken lives, but the thing that he talked about with the utmost horror was not lives that are broken, but lives that are perishing. The loveliest text in all of scripture is "God so loved the world that he gave his only begotten Son, that whoever believes in him should not be wasted, ruined, become utterly useless to God and man, but have everlasting life"—that is the real alternative.

You notice the word "him" in the text: "fear him who destroys body and soul in hell." Who is this "him"? Some people think it refers to the devil, but the devil is one of those who is to be destroyed so it is clearly God. Hell is not something I made for myself, it is something that God is going to do. The scripture is utterly clear on this: God does it, not me.

The next word, working backwards, is "fear". If it is psychologically bad for us to fear hell, why did Jesus tell us to? If you run the danger of pushing people into all kinds of psychological conditions by speaking of hell, why did Jesus do it? He said, "Fear him who is able to do this."

So far, I have only spoken of one text, one statement of our Lord. If that were all there was then it would be quite enough from him, but it is far from all. I must go quickly through the others. In Mark 9, he speaks about those who are thrown into hell "where their worm does not die and the fire is not quenched." He is here saying in this valley on earth the worms do die and the fire is quenched, and it is quenched today. Though the day I walked through that valley a man was burning rubbish in the bottom of it—I have got a slide of that.

The worms did die and the fires did die down. Jesus here says specifically that the worm and the fire do not cease in the place of which he is speaking, and if people cease then why do the worm and the fire go on? I find this an impossible thing to understand. I notice that he speaks of "where their worm does not die," and "where the fire is not quenched". I don't know what the worm and the fire literally are. Treat the language metaphorically as you will, but the reality behind the metaphor is still there to deal with. People have spoken of the worm as the nagging worm of conscience and memory. They can speak how they will; this does not remove the horror of the reality.

The parable of the sheep and the goats is another story that is very well known and is read in many churches on the Sunday at the beginning of Christian Aid Week. I think it could be misunderstood by many as if by doing good deeds to others you save yourself from hell, but that is not the message of the parable. The parable finishes with this statement about the goats: "Depart from me, ye cursed, into the eternal fire which is prepared for the devil and his angels", and "these shall go away into everlasting punishment: but the righteous into life eternal."

The last time I heard that read in church the minister stopped reading just before that verse, but it is part of the story. Those who say that eternal surely cannot mean endless are up against the profound difficulty that almost every other time it is used in the New Testament it does mean endless. God is said to be eternal, Christ is eternal, his salvation is eternal, and in this very verse heaven is eternal. We cannot have it both ways. If hell is temporary then heaven must also be temporary. When the identical word is used of both it becomes very difficult not to give the same meaning to both in the same sentence.

Jesus used other phrases like "weeping and gnashing of teeth" and "outer darkness". They tell me that in the Arctic regions during the winter the most unbearable thing is not the cold, but the lack of light—Jesus spoke of darkness. Finally, I quote one more. Jesus said to his critics, "You shall see Abraham, Isaac, Jacob, and all the prophets in the kingdom and yourselves thrust outside."

He clearly taught that from hell you could see heaven, but not vice versa. In fact, it is physically true about the present

Valley of Gehenna that from the valley you can see the city, but tourists have been right round the city and have come back to England without ever seeing Gehenna, or the Valley of Hinnom. I have spoken to many who have been on Holy Land tours and they think they have seen everything and they have not seen the bottom of this valley, and it was within half a mile of most of the sights they saw. This is the picture that Jesus gives, to know that you are outside it.

That is a pretty horrible picture; it is confirmed in the rest of the New Testament, which I do not go into, I simply quote from Paul's letters where he says that those who know not God or obey not the gospel shall suffer punishment, even eternal destruction. In the book of Revelation, it says they will be tormented day and night forever. The same book speaks of fire and brimstone. Let us look, then, at the alternatives people have suggested in the light of scripture.

Self-imposed suffering. This has nothing whatever to do with what Jesus said was hell. Hell is in the next life, not this one, and it is God who prepares it, not us.

Universal restoration. I find it absolutely impossible to believe that all will somehow be forced into heaven one day in the light of the very clear teaching of our Lord in the Sermon on the Mount, in his parables, and in his direct teaching that hell is not just a possibility or even a probability, but a certainty. The devil and angels are going to be there anyway and all men who have accepted their leadership will join them.

Conditional immortality. I am going to be quite frank here and say that I think a case can be made based on most of the language of scripture that ultimately, after terrible suffering, there could be annihilation, but only after the sufferings of hell. I am afraid I must be honest and say that not all language can be interpreted this way. I am left with the position where, much as I do not like it by nature or by fallen reason, I must accept that Jesus did teach the understanding of hell that Christians for two thousand years have believed.

Faced with this dreadful fact, we are confronted with a simple choice: do we accept the psychologist, the philosopher, the moral ethical teacher, the sentimentalist, and the theologian, on the one hand who all object to this, or do we accept Jesus, believing that he knew the love of God the Father better than any of us, and that since he exercised it in his own life, deep down he knew that this also was the truth? That is the choice. There came a day in my life when I surrendered my reason to his and said, "Jesus, you are not only my Saviour, you are my Lord, and that means my thinking is under your direction as well as everything else." That is why I believe in it today, not because I like it, and I am sure you sense that, but because I believe it to be the truth.

I come, then, to the practical aspect of this. Is this just an academic issue? Is it just a thing to write books about? Is it just a belief about which you can say, "Oh well, you believe it, I don't, let's get on with being a Christian"? The answer is, if it is true then the most profound results come, first of all, to the unbeliever. If you study the lives of preachers like Wesley and Spurgeon, you will find that they did not hesitate to plead with people to come to Christ to save them from hell, because it was real and because they hated the thought of a single soul going there, they preached all the more earnestly.

Now let us ask if there are certain practical issues here. What is it that takes a man to hell? I find that most people believe that everybody is good as soon as they die—the way they talk, you would think so—and believe that the only people who are in hell are Hitler, Nero, and one or two others like this. What is it, then, that takes a man to hell? According to an English proverb it is good intentions.

The road to hell is paved with them. What kind of good intentions? This good intention: "I will become a Christian someday"; "I will start going to church when I've got the house decorated"; "I will start reading my Bible when I've a bit more spare time." That is the kind of good intention that paves the road. Doctor A T Pierson, a great minister in the States, said that in his congregation was an American judge and his wife was a Christian, but he was not.

One day, that judge sitting in his pew felt the conviction of God on him and knew that he must decide, and knew that God was very near, and that he could accept Christ there and then, but the following week he was seeing a bill through the American government and his future career depended on the bill going through, and he knew in his heart that it was a bill that a Christian could not support. The judge was at the crossroads of life. Either this bill would go through and his career would progress or he would accept Christ. Do you know what he decided that Sunday? He decided he would become a Christian after the bill had gone through, but he never did. Twenty years later he died still no nearer to Christ. He had the intention, but when the crisis came he turned it down.

The road to hell is paved with such good intentions. If ever God speaks to you and you know you should get on your knees somewhere privately and say, "Lord Jesus, I know that I deserve hell and I know that I'm going there unless you do something for me and I ask you to save me," then I beg you to do it when the impulse comes.

According to my Bible, here are some of the things that can drag a man down to hell: jealousy, envy, anger, drunkenness, filthy talking, hypocrisy, cowardice, covetousness, lying, and fornicating. Here is a list of things, every one of which according to the New Testament is enough to drag a man there, which is why Jesus said, "if thy right hand offend thee, cut it off, and cast it from thee: for it is profitable for thee that one of thy members should perish, and not that thy whole body should be cast into hell."

He is not being literal because naturally if you cut one hand off you have still got another, and if you take one eye out you have still got a second. What he is saying is that if there is anything you are looking at, anything you are doing with your hand, anywhere your feet take you that is leading you into this then cut it right out. Better to live a narrow life and to be called narrow without this than to go with it to hell.

My next word is "how". How does a man escape from hell? The answer is very simple, it is at the cross that hell becomes most real. I think that those who don't believe in hell don't ever study the cross. Two aspects of the cross tell me this: first, what awful necessity demanded that Jesus die before God could forgive me? What terrible thing was it that made the blood of Jesus Christ the only sufficient price to save me? That answer is hell was the awful necessity.

The second question is what awful experience did Jesus go through for me? The answer is he went through hell. If you want to know what hell is then listen to the Son of God crying, "My God, my God, where are you? Why is it so dark? Why have you left me? Why is there nothing, no sense of your presence?" It was the first time he had ever felt that in all of eternity. That was hell and he was going through it to save us. The cross is the greatest proof of God's love of the sinner and hatred of sin.

There is a hymn that was written by Charles Wesley that I think sums it up perfectly. It goes like this:

> "Love moved him to die and on this we rely, he hath loved, he hath loved us. We cannot tell why, but this we can tell, he hath loved us so well as to lay down his life to redeem us from hell."

Isn't that a wonderful verse? If you don't believe in hell then I ask you, why did Jesus need to go through hell for you? If you don't believe there was this awful possibility why did he have to die? It is impossible to find an answer.

My last word is very practical, and it is to Christians. If what I have said is true then the priority of every Christian is to win others for Christ. Whatever else we do for other people this must be our main task. One of the most disturbing features of the past few decades is the declining interest in saving souls and the abounding enthusiasm in feeding bodies. I want to speak very carefully here, because during Christian Aid Week we are asked to give and to collect for starving bodies. That is right and proper that you should.

Someone who can see someone hungry and not do something about it is not a Christian, but mission societies are having great difficulty in getting money to save souls. During the nineteenth century, Christians in this country poured out man and money in increasing numbers to the world at large. It was the greatest export that Britain has ever made. Why did they do it? Because they believed they were helping to save people from hell.

The last century saw the decline of the belief in hell. It was not that the missionaries neglected the bodies or minds of people when they went out—they built their schools and hospitals—but their aim in going was to save souls. They knew that even if you feed a man every day of his life in this world you have not helped him permanently until you have saved his soul. I just put in a plea that we balance our activity as Christians. The world will give to Christian Aid, the world will give to feed the starving, but only Christians seek to save souls. We are the only people to do this for a lost world and our missionary interest will be directly related to our belief in the things that I have been writing about in this chapter.

While we do give to help those who suffer in body, and while we give to feed the minds, if we really believe this then the effect on Christians is to get our priorities right, and to make evangelism our prime activity and missionary interest—the first call on our purse. It is very practical; it is very down to earth.

Chapter 6

Further Questions

Read Mark 12:13–34

I am going to begin this chapter by answering some questions that I received. The first question is one I cannot answer, nor can anybody. It is a very simple question:

"Where is hell?"

I once heard an answer to that question, which was this: hell is anywhere outside of heaven. Now that is not a bad definition and if you think it through, it has a profound truth in it because, as we said in the previous chapter, to be in hell is to be outside of heaven, to be outside of God. As Jesus said, "You will see yourselves thrust out," and it is almost a picture of somebody standing in a cold, dark street looking in through a lighted window and seeing others having a party inside. This is the kind of picture I get from our Lord's teaching, but I would say anywhere outside of heaven.

If somebody wants to locate it on a map of the universe, the answer is I can't do so, and I can't locate heaven for the very simple reason that when somebody said to Jesus, "Will you put it on a map for us? Will you tell us where heaven is and then we can get there?" Jesus' reply was, "You don't need to know. I will take you." Similarly, with hell I would say you don't need to know because he will send those who are going there to the place itself, but in fact we can't locate it in the universe. We know that places are being prepared, both heaven and hell, but where they are, I can't answer.

"Does time as we know it mean anything to those who have died in the Lord?"

From one point of view, time is an elastic thing in that sometimes time flies and sometimes it drags. Sometimes a twenty-minute sermon seems like an hour; sometimes an hour-long sermon can seem like twenty minutes, though that is less common. It depends on the seat you are sitting on to a degree. I do believe that time will go on in eternity. There is a text in the Authorised Version of the book of Revelation which has misled a lot of people: "there should be time no longer". What is being said in that text is that God is going to proceed immediately with the next step. He will wait no longer to do the next thing.

It does not mean that there will be no time in eternity and, indeed, the biblical idea of eternity is really endless time. To be conscious at all, you must be in time, because to be conscious is to be conscious of what is happening now, what happened then, and what is going to happen in a moment. There is this progressiveness of time. You cannot be conscious without some kind of consciousness of passing moments. Time never moves in a reverse direction. It is always from the past through the present to the future. God is a God of time. Rather than say God is in time, I would say that time is in God, but he is always described to us as a God of time, eternal time. The God who was, and the God who is, and the God who is to be—always in that order, never the reverse. Having said that, God experiences time so differently, not because it doesn't exist, but because to him a thousand years is as one day and one day is as a thousand years. The Bible never says that time means nothing to him. It always says that time is different to him, and I presume that therefore when we share God's glory in heaven, time will be different to us.

Now, about those who have died in the Lord, presumably the questioner is thinking of those who have died and are awaiting the resurrection. How much does time mean to anyone? Well, I have told you that I believe they are conscious with the Lord and that therefore time does mean to anyone?, but whether it means the same thing to them as it does to us, I would question. I would think the interval between death and resurrection to them will go so quickly, because it will be so wonderful. When you are with someone you love, time tends to go rather more quickly than under other circumstances. So, I am speculating, but I would think that time does mean something to them, but that they are with the Lord and therefore the time will be oh so quick until we all join them.

"What rewards will there be in heaven?"

Well, all kinds of rewards. There will be visible rewards. Certain crowns will be worn by certain people. Certain visible tokens of certain special things they have done for the Lord; for example, there is promised in scripture a martyr's crown. Those who have died for the faith will be honoured for this and they will be recognised in heaven. That will be a reward for their death for the Lord. There will be other crowns and you can list them all if you go through them in the scriptures. There is a crown, for example, for those who have kept the faith all the way through, against all the odds, against all the difficulties. There would seem to be a crown for those who have responded to God's grace and become holy while they are here.

There are also rewards of particular responsibilities and positions. This does not mean that we are not equally saved and taken by grace to heaven, but it does mean that there will be differences of responsibility. Those who have been faithful here will be given considerable responsibility there, just as in an earthly firm, if you do a good job in the little office at the bottom you will find yourself promoted. This kind of reward is offered to those who are faithful, especially those who are faithful in jobs that nobody sees but the Lord. There does seem to be a special reward for the things that you have done on earth in secret for God. Jesus was always saying, "Do it in secret and your father who sees in secret will reward you openly." One of the real tests of our Christian life is how much we are prepared to work hard at our Christian living in secret. One thing that is quite certain is that we shall get a lot of surprises in heaven. There will be some pretty big rewards for people we hardly noticed on earth for the things that they did secretly for God. He will reward openly.

If people say that rewards are immoral, then they are flying in the face of our Lord Jesus. If rewards are wrong, then Jesus was wrong to offer them, but you will find again and again that you are blessed when you are persecuted. You are in line with the prophets and the martyrs and great is your reward in heaven. He constantly used this incentive, and Christians are those who accept the incentive of rewards in heaven, but there will be many other rewards of which I know nothing.

"Thinking of thalidomide children born without limbs, will the resurrection of the body mean that their heavenly body will be the same?"

Jesus bore the marks of his crucifixion in his risen body. The body of the Lord Jesus after his resurrection did bear the nail prints, that is perfectly true. They were there for purposes of recognition, but they were also there for purposes of honour and, indeed, I hope that they will stay there for all eternity. Those marks will be very wonderful to us all. I believe that they will be there when he comes back again and we shall look on him who was pierced.

Those are marks that he gained in the service of God. Paul talks about bearing in his body the marks of the Lord Jesus—marks, lashes, scars that he got when he was stoned and whipped for being a Christian. I believe, and this is my own opinion, that those marks which we gain through service for the Lord will remain, without pain or handicap or discomfort, but will be there as a mark of honour. Indeed, when they have been gained in the service of the Lord, they are honourable scars. They would, I think, be of the same category as the nail prints, but I also believe, as I indicated when I was interviewing Matt, that in fact our resurrection body will be a perfect body. I do believe that physical handicaps we have had here through no fault of our own will be overcome in that new body. We shall all be able to see and hear perfectly and our faculties will be complete, and so insofar as the question concerns that kind of handicap, I believe that will be different.

The verse asked about in 1 Corinthians is 15:29, "If the dead will not be raised, what point is there in people being baptised for those who are dead? Why do it unless the dead will someday rise again?" What does this mean? Paul is not, I believe, here referring to a Christian practice, but to a pagan practice. He is holding up to Christians, as our Lord did, pagans with their practices as an example of greater faith than the Christians have. He is trying to get across to Christians that they are showing less faith in the future than pagans do who have this practice of baptising people on behalf of the dead, just in case they died un-baptised. That is why he carefully does not say that is what you mean when you get baptised for the dead, or that is not what we mean. He says, "That is what they mean," and you will find in those few verses that he is speaking about the pagan world and their attitudes to death and their attitudes to resurrection and he is saying, "They have some belief in the future or they wouldn't do what they're doing, and you are denying the resurrection of the dead, so you should have at least as much faith as the pagans."

"What happens to babies and young children when they die?"

The answer is I do not know, and the Bible does not say. All kinds of speculation has occurred and all kinds of answers have been given by Christians. There are some who have dared to say that young children all go to hell when they die. There are others who have said that provided they are baptised, they won't, but will go to *Limbus Infantum* (limbo). Others have said that those go to limbo who are unbaptised babies and that baptised babies go to heaven. All kinds of ideas have come. Some say all babies go to heaven because they haven't sinned yet and therefore are innocent. Others say that all babies go to heaven even though sin is born in them. The blood of Christ covers them.

All this is speculation and the only thing that I can say is this: I am quite sure that whatever God does with babies and young children who die, he will do the right thing. I know God well enough to trust him to do that, and if a child of mine died, I would say to God, "For some reason known to yourself, you have allowed this to happen. I'm content to leave my child in your hands to do whatever you see is right and I know that one day when I learn what you have done, I will see that it was absolutely right." If you believe in a good God, you can believe nothing else, but I think it's better to rest in that than to start making speculative statements that are not backed up by scripture, because that would not be finally the deepest comfort.

"During your conversation with Mr Matthews, you gave me the impression that a Christian could not commit suicide. Is it possible?"

The answer is that it is possible, and under extreme pressure and provocation any of us is capable of doing this. Perhaps many of us have from time to time found that the thought was just played with in our minds. But I think a Christian has even more reason than anyone else for not doing such a thing, for it would be robbing God, as well as self, of something that God gave to be used for his glory. A Christian knows that such an act is no way out of the problem at all and indeed could lead to shame and embarrassment at the coming of Christ. "Why did you take from me the life that I gave you to use for my glory?" A Christian has many, many more reasons for not contemplating such a thing.

Furthermore, a Christian rightly related to a Christian fellowship would surely, long before they reach that point, go and share this burden with some other Christian and find someone who could help them to face whatever was causing such distress to them. It is possible, but I think statistically, it is far, far less probable, and indeed the Lord has his own way of giving us the grace and the courage to face whatever is too much for us. But I would not like to leave the impression that it is impossible, but rather assure the one who asked the question and anyone else that the Lord is the one to turn to long before that stage is reached, and other Christians are there to help. The Samaritans are, as you know, dedicated to helping people who feel that there is no answer to their problems but this.

"Are there to be no families in heaven?"

The answer is there is to be only one. Earthly family circles will not be circles as such in heaven. That is what our Lord's words meant to the Sadducees. They asked who was going to be the husband. They said it was going to be a funny household with seven husbands and one wife and there would be interminable arguments. This was the kind of thing they were saying. They were trying to trap him because they didn't believe that you would survive to see heaven, so they were trying to make heaven sound ridiculous. People who don't believe in the afterlife try to make it sound ridiculous, but in fact Jesus made it quite clear that earthly family relationships apply to this life only.

Somebody asked me recently, "How could I be happy in heaven with my family in hell?" The answer is all your family will be in heaven, the only family you will have then, and your spiritual relationships will be your family relationships there. While we are here we have a deep responsibility for our physical relatives, and we may be the one person who can help them. We ought to keep in touch with all our physical relatives while we are here, but in heaven there will only be one family. My wife and I will be brother and sister in heaven and brother and sister with everybody else in heaven; one family, with one elder brother, Jesus Christ, and one Father, so that will be the relationship.

I find even on earth that I begin to think this way and I find myself closer, much closer, to my spiritual relatives than I am to some of my physical relatives. Don't you find the same? Well, if that gets deeper and deeper until finally it reaches perfection that would be the family in heaven. I am a bit disturbed when people say that they look forward to heaven more because they are going to meet a husband or wife or relative they have loved and lost than because they are going to meet Jesus. I think we need to grow in grace to the point where we see that Jesus is the one we want to meet more than anyone else and the loved ones we meet will be in him, brothers and sisters in him—one family.

"It is obvious that the disciples held a current popular view of reincarnation, otherwise they could not have asked whether a man could be born blind by reason of his own sin. Why did not Jesus give a categorical denial of this idea as he did with other false doctrine, for example, the Sadducees' denial of resurrection?"

I am not sure what reference is referred to here. If it is the story of the man born blind in John's Gospel, Jesus gave a categorical denial of their false assumption, but I don't think their false idea in that case was reincarnation. They asked whether the man was blind because of his own sin, or because of his parents' sin. Now, of course, blindness in the Middle East is a very common disease. Often it is caused by lack of hygiene, but equally often it is caused by diseases that are often a result of the sin of the parents. This happens in this country to a lesser degree.

They were asking a question about the effects of sin on another generation, but they were not asking about reincarnation and I have not come across any belief that the disciples had in reincarnation. Certainly, it was a popular idea then, and when Jesus said to the disciples, "Who do people say that I am?" they said, "Well, some think you're Elijah back again; some think you're John the Baptist," and that was reincarnation, but, of course, the real truth was incarnation. So, Jesus gave a categorical denial to the assumption that a man's blindness is always due to sin, and he denied that this was so and taught them to look at it from quite a different viewpoint.

"What does the 'second death' mean in Revelation 20:14?"

Well, it means the death of the soul as well as of the body. Now, let us understand that death in scripture does not mean to disappear. It does not mean annihilation. It does not mean extinction. It means a condition in which you are no longer in touch with that which gives life. When the body dies, the person has not ceased to be, but physically they are now out of touch with that which gave them physical life—not just breathing life, but life with all its interest, with all its possibilities. When a person dies, they are now out of touch with that which gave them earthly life. The second death is when a person is put out of touch with all that gives them heavenly life, and it is an experience, a distressing and terrible experience far worse than the first death, which people who reject the gospel of Christ will have to face. Can I give you a conundrum here linking up with the last question? If a man is born twice, he will only die once; if he is only born once, he will die twice. That is a summary of the gospel.

"What will souls do in hell?"

That I cannot tell you in detail; I think one could say suffer, but clearly the suffering includes mental remorse and memory of opportunities that have gone by forever. That is our Lord's teaching. I don't think I could say much more than that.

"Once in, can souls ever get out?"

My own understanding of the scripture is no.

"What is the purpose of God in keeping those in hell alive?"

The purpose basically is retribution. The purpose basically is justice. The purpose basically is punishment.

If we reject all retribution and all idea that punishment

is wrong, then of course we are left with a real problem. Now, I know there are problems with that question, and I do not pretend that I find it easy to answer, but that is surely the purpose. It is not to reform them, for they are beyond reforming. It is not used as a deterrent because by then the opportunity to make their choice will have gone. So, of the three purposes of punishment, which are deterrence, reformation, and retribution, two must be knocked out straight away and we are left with the third, which can be the only one.

"Those that believe in Christ have eternal life. Surely that may mean that unbelievers cannot have eternal life in hell, but will perish."

The word "eternal" means not only quantity but also quality. It means both. It means not only everlasting but also real, abundant life. Therefore, whenever you believe, you have come to have everlasting life now. True, you have now got a life that will go on forever. You have a relationship with God that can last forever, but it is life of a particular quality, and this word "eternal" indicates the quality of life. There is such a thing in the Bible as eternal death, and as I have said already, death is a state, not so much of ceasing to be as of being ruined, and the word "perish" means exactly the same thing as the questioner quotes.

"'Faith without works is dead.' 'Faith without works justifies.' These are quotes from James and Romans. Romans 7:25, 'with the mind I myself serve the law of God; but with the flesh the law of sin'. If hell is a place of eternal torment is one saved from it merely by a mental acceptance of Christ, merely by faith; or are works required?"

I would want to spend a whole sermon on this. It is so important an issue. What does James mean by faith, and what does he mean by works? What does Paul mean? They mean two different things by works, and until you see this you will miss the whole point.

James is not saying, "Faith without good deeds is dead." He is saying, "Faith without actions is dead." That is a very different thing, and what he means by faith and works is a faith that acts on what it believes. He gives two examples: Abraham offering Isaac, which was certainly not a good deed to somebody else, and Rahab the harlot welcoming the spies into Jericho. What James is saying is this: "If faith is only mental acceptance and you never act on it, it's not faith."

That is why my children used to play a little game with me. They climbed three or four steps up the stairs and said, "Daddy, play faith." I went and stood at the bottom of the stairs and held my hands behind my back and they jumped to see whether I caught them. Quite a cruel game, isn't it? In fact, of course, I always did, and the hands jumped out and caught them, but the point is, they had to jump before my hands came out. This is faith. A prayer meeting for rain was once held and one little girl went to the prayer meeting with an umbrella. That was faith. Faith that doesn't act is dead.

In other words, faith is something you do with your will. It involves understanding with the mind. It may involve feelings of the heart but essentially it is something you do. You are gambling your future on God. You are launching out onto him. You are saying, "God, I'm just putting my life in your hands. That is a risk, but I am doing it believing that you will catch me and save me." That is real faith, and James is saying, "Faith without that kind of action is useless," because the devils believe mentally that God exists, but they don't act on it.

When Paul talks about faith without works he is speaking of works of the law, good deeds, keeping the

Ten Commandments. He is speaking of something quite different. He is saying that it is faith alone, not trying to do good, that saves you. He would have agreed with James that faith must be active, and he would also go on to say that if faith is real, it will issue in love and good deeds, but he is very carefully protecting us against the most common misunderstanding that if you do good deeds you will get to heaven. It is very important that we should have a clear grasp of this. "Faith without actions is dead." If it is faith with actions, sooner or later it will issue in good deeds as well, but it is not the good deeds that save. It is not the works of the law that save.

"1 Timothy 1:20, "delivered unto Satan, that they may learn not to blaspheme". Is this in any way anything to do with hell?"

No, it is believing that Satan has the power to bring disease and death to a person who is delivered into his power. I think that is another subject, but it has nothing to do with hell.

"Is there no connection between Luke 12:5, 'Fear Him who, after He has killed, has power to cast into hell', and Hebrews 2:14, 'that through death He might destroy him who had the power of death, that is, the devil'"?

I think the questioner is asking whether I was wrong in saying that he who destroys body and soul in hell isn't the devil.

No, I don't believe I was wrong in this. I think Luke 12 is concerned with God, because among those who are destroyed in hell is the devil. It is not as if hell is something that the devil controls and he deals with people. It is something which God controls. The scripture never says, "Well now, there's somebody put into the devil's hell." It is rather, "There's somebody put into hell with the devil." The devil is just one of others. He is not in charge of the place. He does not punish. He is among the punished and I think it is very important to keep this distinction. Hebrews 2 talks about Jesus destroying him that had the power of death, the devil, and, of course, he has destroyed his power and can already liberate people from the bondage of the fear of death because people know that death brings them to Christ, not the devil. Therefore, in a sense, when death comes it is a help and not a hindrance to my spiritual pilgrimage. It is no longer an enemy.

"What were the resurrected bodies of Lazarus and Jairus's daughter like; like Jesus or not?"

The answer is, not like Jesus. They were bodies that went on growing old that finally died again and went back to the grave. In fact, their bodies were what I would call "resuscitated bodies— the kind of resuscitation that happens now on the operating theatre table when somebody is brought back to life after their heart has stopped for a short time. They are brought back into this old body which is then subject to disease again, tiredness, fatigue, old age and death. However, our Lord's body was not that kind of body. He was the first to have the new resurrection body, which is immortal, but their bodies must have been different to that degree.

"When you die, are you judged immediately?"

No, you are not. You must wait, as everybody else must, until the great Day of Judgment.

"If someone who was once a Christian dies without a faith, what happens?"

Someone who was once a Christian dies without a faith. There is a problem here. The evidence of the New Testament about the question, "Can you ever cease to be a Christian having once been one?" is ninety-five per cent in favour of the answer, "No." Once you have been saved, you are saved forever.

I say ninety-five per cent because there are some passages, notably in Hebrews 6 and Hebrews 10, and one or two other places, that do seem to imply the possibility of what is called the sin of apostasy, of having once accepted Christ and then utterly denying that Christ is the Son of God or the Saviour or that his blood can cleanse sin—utterly to deny the whole gospel. There are passages which seem to say that if you reach the point where you absolutely deny Christ and say he is not the Son of God and not the Saviour and doesn't save anyone from hell there is the possibility that this is a sin unto death, as the Apostle John calls it. Now, I say it is about five per cent, and I would preach the ninety-five per cent ninety-five per cent of the time. I would tend to take that as my position, but there is a very great difference between this and a Christian slipping away and apparently losing their faith and falling into sin, who still believes that Christ is the Saviour and died for them, but doesn't feel any longer that they belong. That is a completely different thing. That is backsliding. That happens to many, and wonderful is his grace, he has his way of drawing such people back, sometimes long before they die. That is a very different thing. A backslider is not someone who commits apostasy, but apostasy is so to deny the truth of the gospel that, in fact, you are virtually crucifying the Son of God afresh and shutting yourself off from the only truth that can save you. To backslide from the truth while you still know it to be true is one thing, but to utterly deny the truth of the gospel is another and I would say that there are many Christians who die in a state where they have slidden away from Christ. The answer is they will go to be with Christ. It will embarrass them when they meet him that they slipped away from him, but they will be with him. He doesn't let go that easily. I think it is a warning to us all that of the twelve apostles, one was Judas who went to his own place. But Jesus said, "I have kept them," and it is he who keeps us, not we who keep him. He says, "None shall pluck them out of my hand." That is where the emphasis is.

"Did the people of Noah's time really have a second chance when Jesus preached to them in Hades?"

I don't know. He preached to them and I presume he would not have wasted his time preaching to them if there was no possible result of this. So, I am just going to speculate. I think they did, but they alone are the people in scripture who are said to have had this opportunity.

"We shall rejoice to be with other loved ones in heaven one day. Will this joy be tempered or spoiled if perhaps a loved one is not there?"

I have answered that already. All your loved ones will be there.

"If we have a body in the next life shall we see God, he being a spirit, or only Jesus?"

Well, my answer would be there are enough texts in the Bible to tell us that we are going to see God. "Blessed are the pure in heart, for they shall see God." We are told to seek that holiness without which no man shall see the Lord, and again and again we have this promise that one day we shall know God as well as he knows us.

One day we shall no longer see through a mirror dimly, but then face to face. Now, the kind of mirrors I see God in at the moment are these. I see God in the mirror of nature, but it is only a dim reflection of his power and deity. I see God in the Bible, but again it is only a dim reflection, though it is clearer than in the case of nature. I see God in the faces of saints, but once again it is a reflection as in a mirror, darkly. But one day we are going to turn away from the mirrors and we are going to look face to face and see him. Nobody has seen God yet. "No man has seen God at any time," says the Bible, but Jesus has seen him and he has promised that we will. I don't know how bodies can see a spirit, but I believe that God can manage that too.

"If Jesus went down to hell after he died, does this not mean that there must be hope still for those who are there? So many people believed in him but have not asked for his forgiveness in so many words or given themselves to him. Perhaps there is hope for them yet."

There are two questions here. Regarding the first, I don't believe that Jesus went down to hell after he died. I believe that he went to Hades, which is a different thing, or a different place, a different condition. The word Hades refers to the world of departed spirits, so I did not say that Jesus went down to hell. I know the modern English version of the Apostles' Creed says that, but the original version never said that. It is "He descended into Hades." There was hope, I gather, from 1 Peter 3 for those who had been drowned in the days of Noah, but there isn't another text in the Bible to say there is hope for anyone else. Therefore, I dare not offer it.

Now, it says that many people have believed in him but not asked for forgiveness in so many words. To believe in him is not just to believe that he exists, or to believe that there is a person called Jesus, it is to believe in him as your Saviour. Whether you use the right words or not, he understands whether you have believed in him as Saviour, and any other kind of belief in him is not really belief. The devil believes in Jesus in the sense that the devil knows there is a person called Jesus and that he died for the sins of the world and rose again. Satan knows that, but that is not what I understand by believing. If we have not used the right words, but have nevertheless come to him as our Saviour, I am quite sure we don't need a second chance, because we are saved.

"If this is so, does this not indicate a second chance for those having someone baptised on their behalf?"

In referring to those who are baptised for the dead Paul is alluding to a heathen practice, not a Christian one, and he is using an argument against the Christians by referring to a pagan practice. He is saying that they believe in life after death, or they wouldn't get baptised on behalf of the dead. You as Christians ought to believe it even more, yet you're not. He is not arguing for baptism for the dead, so the second part of the question is answered by that too.

I am interested that some churchgoers feel there ought to be second chances. The Bible does not, and it regards this life as an adequate opportunity to respond to the light. I think we will have to be careful if we find ourselves thinking this way.

"If universalism runs contrary to free will, does not also the doctrine of original sin do so, as it implies that all wills are born in bondage to sin and so are not really free?"

That I cannot answer in one minute. It is the whole question of predestination and free will, and I have yet to meet the man who can deal with that quickly.

Let me say that to me the Bible teaches both divine sovereignty, or predestination if you like, and human responsibility, or free will if you like. Both are taught, and therefore I believe in both. I believe that there is divine sovereignty. I believe that there is human responsibility. I think those who believe one or the other would like to rewrite the Bible if they could. I believe both. I find it difficult to line them up logically, but I am prepared to believe that my mind is not quite big enough to do so. As long as I believe both and preach both, that is what I am concerned about.

Now, original sin is not quite the same thing as divine sovereignty. Original sin is the belief which the Bible teaches very simply, and that is that we are not born morally neutral and then either become bad or good. "As we are born, we are born with a bad nature." The Bible is quite clear that we are born like this. It is easier to go down than up. Well, we learn the word "no" before we learn the word "yes". If you have had children you will know the truth of this. You don't really believe in original sin until you have had children and then you see it. It really comes out, and you say, "Where did they get that nature from? It must be from your side, dear." But it comes out and they are born with it.

The question is this: "If I'm born that way, how can I be responsible?" I don't know how, but I know that I am. The Bible again teaches that we are born like this and the Bible also teaches that God holds us responsible for what we do. Again, I cannot line it up logically, but I know that it is true. A man in the RAF said to me, "Padre, if you'd been born into the family I was born into and brought up the way I was brought up, you'd be doing the same things I'm doing." I said, "Well, I think that's probably true, but I would still be ashamed of it, as you apparently are," and he was. You are not ashamed of something when it is not your responsibility. Somehow, I hold these two things together.

"Will we be happy in heaven knowing our loved ones are in hell?"

I dealt with that when I said that in heaven all our loved ones will be the people of God and they will all be there.

"Do you find that an unconverted person seeking Christ will bring up the question of hell?"

A few do, but very few; I have met one or two who did. The funny thing is that it is people who have heard who seem most troubled about those who have not and it is people who are believers in heaven who have the most questions about hell. It is funny, but a man who is really ruining his life, he doesn't seem to find any difficulty in the belief in hell. A man who knows he is doing wrong doesn't seem to have much difficulty in it either, so I can only answer that by saying occasionally, not very often. Most of the questions seem to come from Christians.

"Do you ever bring it up in conversation with such a person?"

That will depend on what the word hell will convey to him. I would want to know what kind of a picture he will have if I use the word. I would certainly want to bring up with such a person that God has said that you reap what you sow, and there is a day of retribution, of reckoning, of coming to your accounts. I would want to bring that idea up rather than the word hell if that was going to bring a false picture into his mind.

"Is it correct that at death all spirits go to Hades, which is divided into paradise for Christians and the prison for unbelievers? If so, then separation, sheep from goats as

it were, comes at death and not at the Judgment."

No, because the separation of the sheep and the goats is prior to the final destinies of heaven and hell if you read the parable carefully. I agree that there is a degree of separation already, but paradise is not the full eternal kingdom that is promised to Christians and neither is the prison hell. For one thing, the devil and his angels are not in Hades. They will be in hell, and there are a number of differences between the second and the third stages of the afterlife. There is a degree of separation, but it is not the ultimate separation between the sheep and the goats.

"If Christ went through hell for us and God can't look upon sin and hell, then how could God lift Christ out of hell?"

There are a number of "ifs" in that, and I'll have to deal with them first. He went through hell, but what I mean is not that he went through the place, but that he went through the experience. He was the only man who went through hell in this life, and when he was on the cross with God away from him, he was going through hell for us. I do believe this. It was not after his death that he went through hell, but before his death in the darkness and the god-forsakenness. God the Father lifted Christ out of Hades, not out of hell. He died, went to Hades, and was raised from there on the third day.

"Is there any comfort for the Christian who is fairly certain that other members of their family, those they love, will go or have gone to hell?"

This is a very real question and a very deep one. The first comfort is that God will always do what is absolutely right and fair by your loved ones. The second comfort is that there is always the possibility that they did believe in God but that you didn't know about it. I think this has happened on a number of occasions, and we might find some surprises in heaven as a result of this. I would say this question, which is a very sincere one, makes it all the more important that we should be concerned about our family before they die, before we are concerned about them afterwards. We have opportunities now which we should take without forcing it down anyone's throat or offending them by pushing it too hard. We should have this concern.

"Is the most terrible thing about hell the fear that the sinner is longing after God and can never reach him rather than the lake of fire, which may be figurative language?"

I do not know what will be the worst thing in hell. I know that it will be terrible. I think the longing after God is not likely to be there because, quite frankly, if a person is longing after God I think that would have started during their life. One of the things that sin does to you is to reduce the longing for God until it is not there at all. I would rather think the hell was that there is no longing after God and there is no sense of God. There might be a longing after heaven, which is a rather different thing.

A man said to me quite recently when I was discussing heaven and hell, "Tell me about heaven," and I am going to tell you about heaven in a moment. When I told him, he said, "You know, that would be hell to me. It really would. I can imagine nothing worse than singing hymns forever with a lot of Christians." He really said it would be hell. Quite frankly, I think we should realise that sin removes the appetite for heaven and that perhaps one of the most terrible things about hell will be that people will not want heaven. I don't know. I am speculating, but I don't know which is the worse thing.

"At the name of Jesus every knee should bow" — Philippians 2:10. Does this mean that after the Day of Judgment even the wicked will submit and acknowledge Christ as Lord?"

The answer is it doesn't mean that. It does mean that when they all see him they will acknowledge him as Lord, but you will notice it does not say they will all say that he is Saviour. Even the devil and the demons will acknowledge that he is Lord, which means that he is King, that he is Boss, that he is Master, but what he is waiting for is somebody to call him Saviour. Calling him Lord is a different thing.

"Will those who are of unsound mind now be taken into heaven and have perfect minds?"

Well, the answer is that I don't know. I must leave such people in God's hands and again I am quite sure that I know God well enough to trust him to do what is best in this case. As we get older, many of us find that our mind can become more feeble, and many great saints have ended their lives without a grip of their mental faculties. I am quite sure they will have perfect minds in glory because, in fact, the reason for the decay of their thinking is purely physical. It is part of the process of decay in the body. Senility is something that belongs to this world. It has nothing to do with the next, and it may well be that other mental illnesses have a similar cure in the next world.

"I was left with the impression that the story of the beggar Lazarus was an accurate illustration of the life immediately after death where they would have no bodies, yet eyes, fingers, and tongue are specifically mentioned. Could you clarify?"

I can answer that one quickly—no, except to say that quite clearly, life after death is conscious and the only way we can imagine being conscious is having faculties. Therefore, the Bible uses faculty language to get across the idea that we shall be conscious. You see, we talk of the eyes of God, the hands of God, the feet of God. Does that mean we literally think he has eyes, he has feet, he has hands? No, it is the only way we can think of conscious personal existence. I would think that is what is mentioned here.

"I understood you to infer that in this state, Satan would be unable to tempt people because he could only tempt us through our bodies and their activities. How does this fit with such things as mental cruelty, rage, deceit, bitterness, et cetera?"

Well, there is no mention of Satan in Hades anywhere in the Bible. He is mentioned in hell at the end. Until the very end, as far as I understand my Bible, Satan is in heaven, not in hell and he doesn't leave heaven until towards the end. In order to contact Satan, it would be necessary to get through to the heavenly realms. Indeed, as soon as you sit in the heavenly places with Christ by faith, you are wrestling with principalities and powers. This is, I think, why Satan does not tempt people or cannot touch them in Hades, but they are what they have become in that state, so again, I don't think I can say more than that.

Think about the answers that I have given to these questions and if you can't find them in the Bible scrap them because my opinion is not worth tuppence. But insofar as some of those questions have been questions to which I don't know of any direct answer in the Bible, I can only share with you the way I have thought about them. Please do not take that as authoritative truth.

FURTHER QUESTIONS

Now I am going to talk to you about heaven.

Read John 14:1–6

I have heard many people object to Christian beliefs about hell, but I have not met many who objected to belief about heaven. I think there is an obvious reason for this, but some people have criticised and attacked our views on heaven. On the one hand, there are those who say it is all a delusion, a fairy tale. It is all of a piece with fairies at the bottom of your garden, and all this talk about pearly gates and golden streets and harps is quite preposterous. Indeed, there has been a spate of jokes about heaven, which have revealed how lightly people have taken the Christian belief in heaven. Most of them are connected with the pearly gates. I don't know if that is a defence against the likelihood of those gates being shut against them, but we have this constant series of jokes about people arriving at the pearly gates. You must have heard some of them.

The Sadducees treated heaven as a joke. They came to Jesus and they said that they could not believe in a heaven. Jesus said that there were three reasons why they found it difficult. The first was that they constantly tried to imagine heaven in earthly terms. That was the first place where they went wrong. Heaven is so different from earth that you can't think of there as like here. Secondly, he told them that they had gone wrong by forgetting the power of God. Now, if we remember the power of God to make this world and the wonder of this life, how much more could he make a heaven? If we think that heaven could not possibly be true, we have forgotten the power of God. Thirdly, Jesus said to the Pharisees that they were judging the heavenly by the earthly—mistake number one. They were forgetting the power of God—mistake number two. And mistake number three was they didn't know the scriptures.

I agree that there is great difficulty in imagining what any other world is like. When they evacuated Tristan da Cunha after the volcanic eruption there, they brought the planeload of Tristan da Cunhans to London. They had never seen a tube train. They had never seen a skyscraper or a house with more than one storey, and they were put in the middle of London. In the photographs of them walking around, their eyes were as big as their faces. They just had no idea that people could live in a place like this and scuttle down holes like rabbits and go along tunnels and pop up again and look up to skyscrapers. They just could not believe it, any more than people who use the Tube and live in the skyscrapers can think of heaven, but that does not mean it is not real. It just means it is difficult to imagine.

There are some who have gone further and said heaven is not only a delusion, it is a drug. The first man to say this was called Charles Kingsley who wrote a book, *Tom and the Water Babies*. Charles Kingsley said, "Religion is the opiate of the people." What he went on to say was that if you get too preoccupied with heaven you are of no earthly use, and that if you are just living up in the clouds all the time, you can become indifferent to the evils of children working in factories and other things which Charles Kingsley fought against—the pantomime children and the chimney sweep boys. There is an element of truth in that, but Charles Kingsley was an Anglican clergyman and he was not saying, "Forget about heaven altogether." He was just saying, "Don't live so much up there that you're no use down here."

It was Karl Marx who took up that saying of Charles Kingsley, the Anglican clergyman, and said again, "Religion is the opiate of the people. Forget heaven altogether and then you can do most good down here." I challenge Karl Marx on this. The people who have often done most for their fellow men down here are those who have believed most intensely in heaven. Do you know that Lord Shaftesbury, who did so much for social reform in this country, had printed on every sheet of note paper this text at the top: "Even so, come, Lord Jesus." He was a man whose thoughts were in heaven, but he was a lot of earthly use.

The thing is to get a balance, but I would say that the church today has fallen for this and we no longer sing about heaven as we used to. I sometimes have a job choosing hymns about heaven and I have to choose a children's hymn such as this one: "There's a home for little children above the bright blue sky." There is nothing wrong in singing a children's hymn sometimes except you become as little children, but I can hardly find any decent hymns on heaven in hymn books. We have stopped talking about it. There was a day when people used to sing, "A tent or a cottage, what do I care? They're building a mansion for me over there." We don't sing like that now. We have fallen for the world's jibe that it's pie in the sky when you die, which I always say is better than pain in the pit when you flit. They have so teased us about heaven and they have so said, "Heaven is just not worth thinking about," that we have become obsessed with this world. Instead of a gospel that saves us for the next, we have talked about a political and social programme that saves us in this.

Now, these two things ought to go together, but the priority must always be the eternal world, so I am unashamedly going to talk to you about heaven. How do we know about heaven? Well, the answer is we have got three first-hand witnesses who have been there and who have told us what it is like. You know, somebody once said to me, "Well, I'd believe in heaven if somebody had been there and come back and told us." Well, there are three people who have and we can go on what they say, and it is quite enough. In fact, everything I know about heaven comes from these three people.

The first man I call as a witness who went to heaven is a man called Paul. You will read the account of his trip in 2 Corinthians 12. Paul says that he knows a man who visited heaven, "whether in the body I do not know, or whether out of the body I do not know, God knows—such a one was caught up to the third heaven. And I know such a man—whether in the body or out of the body I do not know, God knows—how he was caught up into Paradise and heard inexpressible words, which it is not lawful for a man to utter." You read the story. Paul had been there. Here is the second witness, a man called John. A man called John was lying in a prison cell on the little island of Patmos. One Sunday morning as he thought about the Lord, the Spirit took him out of his body and took him up to heaven. He saw a door, and the door opened and he saw right into heaven. He wrote down a very great deal of what he saw. We have got that in the last book in the Bible.

My primary witness is, of course, Jesus himself, because John and Paul visited heaven after Jesus. Jesus was there first. Do you know John 3:16? Do you know what Jesus said just three verses before? He said, "No one has ascended into heaven but he who came down from heaven, even the Son of Man." In other words, "I've come from there. I wasn't always down here. I've come from heaven." And then in verse twelve, the verse before that in John 3, he says this: "If I have told you earthly things, and ye believe not, how shall ye believe, if I tell you of heavenly things?"

Therefore, I would say that if I am prepared to believe what Jesus says about this life, then I must surely be prepared to believe what he says about the next, but if I'm not prepared to believe the one, I'll have problems with the other.

What did these three say about heaven? At this point we have got to use picture language because we are dealing with realities beyond the understanding of our experience. If the

FURTHER QUESTIONS

language is metaphor in picture, that doesn't worry me. It is still reality. I am going to try to answer three questions:

Where is it?

What is it like?

Who will be there?

First of all, where is it? I can't put it on a map. I remember hearing in the late 1960s that we could then go eighty-two million light years into space with our radio telescopes; eighty-two million light years. I don't understand that. I do not know how far that is. My mind cannot understand it. A computer might, but I cannot, and people have said, "And still there's no trace of heaven." People say, "Where is it in the universe?" We say, "Our Father, who art in heaven," and we tend to look up when we say it. Where is that? Eighty-two million light years away at least.

I have the feeling we ought to be thinking in terms of a different dimension altogether, that heaven is much nearer than that, that heaven is all around Earth in a different dimension invisible to us. If Earth is in heaven, as it were; if Earth is surrounded by heaven, then it is true that wherever you are in the universe, you look up in the world, you look up to heaven. It is true that in him we live and move and have our being, and I think of heaven spatially now, as everywhere around Earth in a spiritual dimension, not available to our telescopes or radios, but available to those with eyes to see. "Lord," said Elijah, "open the young man's eyes," and suddenly there just above him were chariots, chariots of God. Heaven was as near as that, and when Yuri Gagarin went up into space and came back saying that he hadn't seen God and he hadn't seen heaven and he hadn't seen angels, which he thought was a great joke, I just wanted to shout back, "Gagarin, God saw you and the angels saw you, but you just weren't moving in heaven. You're just not attuned to this. You just can't see it. Why, every bush is ablaze with God to those who have eyes to see, and to others he's a million miles away."

Where is it then? I don't know. I don't need to know. Thomas asked where it is but Jesus said that he didn't need to know because he would take him. That is what the phrase, "I'm the way," means in Eastern colloquialism. If you say to someone, "I'm the way," what you mean is, "I won't tell you how to get there. I'll come with you and take you there—the quickest way," but let me remind you that heaven, as we are talking of it now, is the distant future of the Christian, the ultimate destiny of the believer. Heaven will include a new earth.

One of the glories to me about heaven will be that it will include the earth. Presumably, as I see it, it will include free space travel for Christians without all the expensive business of rockets—the whole universe available to human beings, freely. This is what I look forward to. Fantastic—maybe, but it is still true. My great grandfather would have said, "It's absolutely fantastic that you believe that three men can go to sleep around the moon." He would have thought I was a lunatic, quite literally, but it is now true. Just because a thing is fantastic it doesn't mean it is not true. I believe that there will be a whole new universe, a new heaven and a new earth, the whole lot, spring cleaned, the whole lot renovated and people in that universe. Furthermore, it is going to have a metropolis, a capital city. We are talking now about building cities out in space, linking up satellites until we have got a city out in space. Well, that is quite marvellous, but God thought of it first and he has promised to do it. He is going to build a space city that according to the Bible is fifteen hundred miles square.

People sometimes tell me that if all the people I think are coming back to life come back to life the place is going to be pretty crowded. Not if we have got a new universe to live in. Not if one capital city is fifteen hundred miles square. You could swallow up the whole of Europe in that. Let us take the Bible language as it stands. Let us not treat it as fairy stories. We are speaking about a new universe and a space city.

"I saw the New Jerusalem coming down out of heaven." You see, everything man builds is from the bottom up. Everything God builds is from the top down. We build our towers of Babel reaching up into the sky but God comes and he builds down and he tells us that here is his city. He is the builder and maker of the place we really want to live in. Planners are still arguing as to what is the ideal layout for a city. They will never get the ideal layout until God sends the New Jerusalem down, and then the planners who are Christians will say, "You know, why didn't I think of that?" That's the ideal city. Well, where is it? I don't know. I only know that Jesus said, "I'll go and prepare it and then I'll come and get you." That is enough for me.

What is it like? I am going to list certain things that will not be there, and certain things that will be there, and that will give you the feel of the place. Let me give you an example. In the heavenly city there will be no sanctuary. Whereas most earthly cities have religious buildings with spires, domes or minarets, there will be no churches, no chapels, no temples in the heavenly city. Why not? Because you will worship God everywhere; you won't need any place to worship in. "I saw no temple there, no sanctuary."

There is one thing I must confess will be a disappointment to me, but the rest will be so wonderful that I will forget about it, I am quite sure. There will be no sea. That is clearly stated. The sea is a threatening enemy of man, and there will be no sea in the new universe. And here is something that will frankly make some people say, "That will be hell": there will be no sex. Sex was given to us for down here. We need it here, but there will be no sex there. For those who have lived for little else, that will be just the opposite of heaven, but you see, there will be true love there for everybody whether they have been married or unmarried here. There will be the fullest love for everybody—no sex.

There will be no suffering, no hospitals, no asylums, no sanatoria, no colonies, no prisons, no refugee camps, no suffering. There will be no separation, either by distance or death, and therefore there will be no sorrow. "God shall wipe away every tear from their eyes." There will be no shadows. We are told that because God is light, the sun and the moon will be obsolete and there will be light everywhere. No dark alleyways, no shadows, no darkness—light; that is why a church down here ought to be a light-filled building. God is light. People talk about a dim religious life. That is thoroughly pagan. We ought to have the brightest possible churches. God is light. Above all—and frankly, this will make it heaven—there will be no sin, no bad temper, no lust, no anger, no jealousy, no envy, no pettiness, no gossip. Can you imagine this? I can't, but there isn't going to be any sin.

Those are the things that will not be there but what will be there? Well, here are certain other things. There will be rest. Now, let me tell you again that this does not mean a lot of armchairs and a kind of large airport lounge. It is amazing how many people think like this. The rest that the Bible talks about is the rest from mental and spiritual frustration. Jesus said, "Come unto me, all ye that labour and are heavy laden," and he was referring to those who were desperately trying to be good enough for God and could not achieve it and were frustrated and hemmed in. He said, "and I will give you rest." The rest of heaven will be busyness, working, serving him day and night, twenty-four-hour shifts, but it will be the kind of rest where you are not frustrated, where you achieve what you want to do, where you are not hemmed in, where you are not feeling "I wish I were better than I am." That will be rest.

There will be rewards, and I spoke about those above last Sunday morning—rewards for special service, for martyrdom and for other things. There will be responsibility and the responsibilities of heaven will be graded according to how faithful you were here. If you carried your responsibilities here well, you will have greater responsibilities there, so there will be grades of responsibility. There will be relationships. I don't know if you have ever thought of this, but you will have a different name in heaven. I won't come over to you and say, "Hello, Charlie Brown," or whatever your name is up there. I won't say that because you won't say, "Hello David Pawson." We shall have new names. We shall be so different from what we are down here. We shall be perfect, meaning that our completely glorified nature will demand a new name, and so we are going to be given new names. I wonder what your name is going to be in glory.

There will be a revelation. There will be no question time up there. We shall understand the answers to all these problems. There will be knowledge and light and revelation and understanding. There will be righteousness there. Not only will there be no sin, there will be goodness, cleanness, uprightness, and holiness. Talk to some people about a place where there is only holiness, and they would say, "That's hell," but it isn't; it is heaven.

There will be rejoicing. I'll tell you what; the choir will be a bit fuller in heaven because you will be in it. I know you may be tone deaf now, or you may only be able to make a joyful noise to the Lord down here, but you will be in the choir there. You will have a glorious voice. One of the first things we are going to do in heaven is learn a new song. We shall also sing the song of Moses as well. If you study the last book in the Bible, you will discover that there is more about singing there than in any other book but the Psalms, as if we are being told that in heaven you will sing, sing, sing. The Hallelujah Chorus comes out of the book of Revelation. There is singing all the way through Revelation, and all of this unending. Now, some people say, "Well, that's going to get terribly boring." Don't you believe it!

I would not like to live here forever, and I would agree with Fred Hoyle, the astronomer, who once said on the radio that if he had his choice, he would like to live for three hundred years. He felt that seventy or eighty years was too short, but that three hundred would be about right. That is because he was on earth. Life is too short for this world. Thank God it is. It should leave us dissatisfied. If life were long enough for this world to do everything that we wanted to do, to explore all that God has made, we should want to stay here longer, but we are frustrated. We groan. We want to prepare for the future because life is too short.

Who will be there? Somebody once said to me, "It's heaven for climate, but hell for company." A lot of the jokes are in that kind of vein. In fact, I would say for company, heaven is the best place. I think one of the most awful things about hell will be the lack of communication between utterly selfish people. The glorious thing about heaven is perfect relationships with each other. Now, who will be there? Heaven is not empty. It will be populated.

There are four things that I would say here. First of all, the saints will be there. A huge family—you will need eternity to get to know them all, but it will be a huge family. It will be a large family, so big that no man could number it. It will be a varied family, every kindred and tribe and tongue. Every colour and race and culture will be represented there. Won't the cultural life in heaven be interesting? Won't the music be interesting? What a varied family and what an interesting family—the prophets, the apostles, the martyrs, the reformers. Which one would you like to meet first? I would give anything to have Paul for an hour there, just to find out what he really meant in certain verses, but then I shall be able to talk to Paul—meet this little man who was such a big missionary; talk to Abraham and Isaac and Jacob and Moses and the apostles. The saints will all be there, all your spiritual relatives and you will have no others.

Secondly, the angels will all be there. It is getting quite crowded. There are myriads upon myriads of them. If you have never believed in angels before, you will believe in them then, because you will meet them and you will share heaven with them. The amazing thing is that at the moment the angels are a little bit above us, but in heaven we shall be a little bit above them. God's will is that we should be reversed and we are told that the angels will serve us in heaven. I don't know if you have ever had the luxury of having servants on earth, but you will have them in heaven—angels to serve you.

The Lamb will be there. Jesus will be there. What will he look like? I don't know. We will see the nail prints in his hands. I have often wondered what he looks like. I have never been satisfied with any picture. I once collected picture postcards, copies of all the portraits of Jesus that have ever been painted. I got up to thirty, and I looked at them all and I said, "Not one of them is right," so I did one of my own in pastels. I put weeks of work into that. I did it and I tore it up and threw it away. What does he look like? We shall see him as he is. He will be there.

Above all, God the Father will be there. It is the Father's home, and children love coming home, especially to a loving Father like this. To the godly person, I think the most wonderful thing of all will be that it is the Father's home. Baden Powell was a man who had a real Christian faith. When he died, he was buried and they put on his tombstone his name and his dates, and then they just put a circle with a dot in the middle. Do you know what that means? If you were a Boy Scout, you will know what that means. It is a tracking sign, and it means "gone home". If you want to find me now, you will have to come to my home. Over every Christian's grave you could just put that—gone home.

Well, I have taken you through death, the intermediate state, the resurrection of the body, the judgment of the nations, hell. Now we are in heaven. I want to finish by reading you a text from the book of Deuteronomy. It is something Moses said just before he died, and this is what he said to all the children of Israel: "I call heaven and earth to record this day against you, that I have set before you life and death, blessing and cursing: therefore choose life, that both thou and thy seed may live".

I wanted to finish with that text because I have not just been talking about academic things. I have also been talking about your future and mine. I finish with these words of Moses because in a sense what he was doing for the children of Israel I have tried to do for you in a simple way. I call heaven and earth to witness against you this day that I have set before you the two alternative futures that await every man and woman—life or death, blessing or curse, heaven or hell. Therefore, I say choose life that you may live.

What does that say to me? It says this: first, that the Bible is right and that there are only two destinies; second, that you don't choose between them. The only choice you can make is to choose heaven. You need do nothing to go to the other place. I once saw a poster outside a church, which was a bit blunt, but it said the truth, and it was this: "The road to hell keeps straight on; the road to heaven, right-about turn." That is the truth. The choice you need to make is to choose heaven, to choose life. Nobody ever finished in heaven by accident. Many people finished in hell that way, or will do by good intentions and the rest, or just by neglecting so great a salvation. You choose life.

Well then, how do you choose to go to heaven? By trying to live a good life? No. You only get two-thirds of the way, and that is not enough. By trying to be religious? No. By joining a church? No. By getting baptised? No. By taking holy communion? No. Although all of those have their place. How do you choose life? By choosing Jesus, that is how, and by realising that he went through hell that we might go to heaven, that he was made a curse that we might be blessed, that he died that we might live, and that what the cross is all about is this: he died that we might be forgiven. He died to make us good, that we, at last, might go to heaven, saved by his precious blood.

I just hope that the day will come when we will look around and see the members of our congregation in glory—not one missing. To see each other there forever will be just heaven in the presence of Christ. What I would hate to feel would be that anyone should face Christ one day and have him say to them, "But you knew what to do. You knew what the future held. You went to Commercial Road Baptist Church in Guildford and you heard the truth and you knew what you could do about it."

Let us pray: Oh God, our loving heavenly Father, you have done everything that needed to be done to open the kingdom of heaven to us, and we thank you that the gates fling wide to all believers. We know that in your kingdom you will only have beggars, those who come and ask for mercy, and we pray that you will enable us to realise that our future depends upon what we do about your words, that when the great day comes and you call your people to glory, we may not be missing. We ask it in Jesus' name and for his sake. Amen.

BOOKS BY DAVID PAWSON
AVAILABLE FROM DAVIDPAWSON.COM

BIBLE COMMENTARIES

UNLOCKING THE BIBLE Omnibus ISBN 978 0 007166 66 4
UNLOCKING THE BIBLE - Charts, diagrams and images ISBN 978 1 911173 17 5

Introducing GENESIS ISBN 978 1 911173 80 9
Introducing The OLD TESTAMENT and HEBREW POETRY ISBN 978 1 911173 90 8

A Commentary on GENESIS Chapters 1-25 ISBN 978 1 911173 82 3
A Commentary on EXODUS ISBN 978 1 911173 85 4
A Commentary on Selected PSALMS ISBN 978 1 911173 91 5
A Commentary on ECCLESIASTES ISBN 978 1 911173 98 4
A Commentary on ISAIAH ISBN 978 1 913472 05 4
A Commentary on JEREMIAH ISBN 978 1 911173 76 2
A commentary on DANIEL ISBN 978 1 911173 06 9
A Commentary on THE MINOR PROPHETS ISBN 978 1 911173 94 6
A Commentary on ZECHARIAH ISBN 978 1 911173 38 0

A Commentary on the Gospel of MATTHEW ISBN 978 1 913472 09 2
A Commentary on the Gospel of MARK ISBN 978 1 909886 26 1
A Commentary on the Gospel of LUKE ISBN 978 1 911173 21 2
A Commentary on the Gospel of JOHN ISBN 978 1 909886 27 8
A Commentary on ACTS ISBN 978 1 909886 38 4
A Commentary on ROMANS ISBN 978 1 909886 78 0
A Commentary on 1 & 2 CORINTHIANS ISBN 978 1 909886 95 7
A Commentary on GALATIANS ISBN 978 1 909886 29 2
A Commentary on EPHESIANS ISBN 978 1 909886 98 8
A Commentary on PHILIPPIANS ISBN 978 1 909886 74 2
A Commentary on COLOSSIANS ISBN 978 1 913472 17 7
A Commentary on 1 & 2 THESSALONIANS ISBN 978 1 909886 73 5
A Commentary on 1 & 2 TIMOTHY, TITUS, PHILEMON - The Personal Letters ISBN 978 1 909886 70 4
A Commentary on HEBREWS ISBN 978 1 909886 33 9
A Commentary on JAMES ISBN 978 1 909886 72 8
A commentary on 1 & 2 PETER ISBN 978 1 909886 79 7
A Commentary on the LETTERS OF JOHN ISBN 978 1 909886 69 8
A Commentary on JUDE ISBN 978 1 909886 28 5
A Commentary on the book of REVELATION ISBN 978 1 909886 25 4

EXPLAINING SERIES
A CHRISTIAN DISCIPLESHIP TRAINING PROGRAMME

THE AMAZING STORY OF JESUS ISBN 978 1 911173 29 8
THE RESURRECTION: The Heart of Christianity ISBN 978 1 911173 30 4
STUDYING THE BIBLE ISBN 978 1 911173 31 1
NEW TESTAMENT BAPTISM ISBN 978 1 911173 33 5
BEING ANOINTED AND FILLED WITH THE HOLY SPIRIT ISBN 978 1 911173 18 2
ETERNALLY SECURE? What the Bible says about being saved ISBN 978 1 911173 19 9
GRACE AND SALVATION: Generous, Undeserved, Co-Operation ISBN 978 1 911173 99 1
THE KEY STEPS TO BECOMING A CHRISTIAN ISBN 978 1 911173 87 8
THE TRINITY ISBN 978 1 911173 07 6
HOW TO STUDY A BOOK OF THE BIBLE: JUDE ISBN 978 1 911173 34 2
THE TRUTH ABOUT CHRISTMAS ISBN 978 1 911173 77 9
END TIMES ISBN 978 1 911173 46 5
WHAT THE BIBLE SAYS ABOUT WORK ISBN 978 1 911173 36 6
WHAT THE BIBLE SAYS ABOUT MONEY ISBN 978 1 911173 35 9
GRACE: Undeserved Favour, Irresistible Force or Unconditional Forgiveness?
ISBN 978 1 909886 84 1
THREE TEXTS OFTEN TAKEN OUT OF CONTEXT: Expounding the truth and exposing error
ISBN 978 1 909886 85 8
BUILDING A NEW TESTAMENT CHURCH ISBN 978 1 911173 69 4
DE-GREECING THE CHURCH: The impact of Greek thinking on Christian beliefs
ISBN 978 1 911173 20 5

TOPICAL BOOKS

Angels ISBN 978 1 909886 02 5
A Preacher's Legacy ISBN 978 1 911173 27 4
By God, I Will - The Biblical Covenants ISBN 978 1 909886 21 6
Christianity Explained ISBN 978 1 909886 64 3
Completing Luther's Reformation ISBN 978 1 911173 26 7
Defending Christian Zionism ISBN 978 1 909886 31 5
Heaven and Hell: A message of hope and warning to believers ISBN 978 1 913472 25 2
Is John 3:16 the Gospel? ISBN 978 1 909886 62 9
Israel in the New Testament (includes Galatians) ISBN 978 1 909886 57 5
Jesus Baptises In One Holy Spirit ISBN 978 1 909886 66 7
JESUS: The Seven Wonders of HIStory ISBN 978 1 909886 24 7
Kingdoms in Conflict ISBN 978 1 909886 04 9
Leadership Is Male ISBN 978 1 909886 67 4
Living in Hope ISBN 978 1 909886 65 0
Loose Leaves from My Bible ISBN 978 1 909886 55 1
Men for God ISBN 978 1 913472 20 7
Not As Bad As The Truth (David's Autobiography) ISBN 978 1 913472 35 1
Once Saved, Always Saved? ISBN 978 1 913472 27 6
Practising the Principles of Prayer ISBN 978 1 909886 63 6
Remarriage is Adultery Unless ... ISBN 978 1 909886 22 3
Simon Peter: The Reed and the Rock ISBN 978 1 909886 23 0
The Character of God ISBN 978 1 909886 34 6
The Challenge of Islam to Christians ISBN 978 1 913472 34 4
The God and the Gospel of Righteousness ISBN 978 1 909886 68 1
The Lord's Prayer ISBN 978 1 909886 71 1
The Maker's Instructions - A new look at the 10 Commandments
ISBN 978 1 909886 30 8
The Normal Christian Birth ISBN 978 1 913472 36 8
The Road To Hell ISBN 978 1 909886 59 9
Tributes by Friends of David Pawson ISBN 978 1 913472 21 4
Understanding the Resurrection ISBN 978 1 911173 22 9
Understanding the Second Coming ISBN 978 1 911173 23 6
Understanding Water Baptism ISBN 978 1 911173 24 3
What the Bible says about the Holy Spirit ISBN 978 1 909886 54 4
What I'm Looking Forward To: Life After Life After Death ISBN 978 1 913472 26 9
When Jesus Returns ISBN 978 1 913472 33 7
Where has the Body been for 2000 years? - Church history for beginners
ISBN 978 1 909886 20 9
Where is Jesus Now? ISBN 978 1 911173 78 6
Why Does God Allow Natural Disasters? ISBN 978 1 909886 58 2
Word And Spirit Together ISBN 978 1 909886 60 5

www.ingramcontent.com/pod-product-compliance
Lightning Source LLC
Chambersburg PA
CBHW070109120526
44588CB00032B/1401